Prototype

Prototype

Design and Craft in the 21st Century

Edited by Louise Valentine

BLOOMSBURY

LONDON • NEW DELHI • NEW YORK • SYDNEY

Bloomsbury Academic
An imprint of Bloomsbury Publishing Plc

50 Bedford Square	1385 Broadway
London	New York
WC1B 3DP	NY 10018
UK	USA

www.bloomsbury.com

Bloomsbury is a registered trade mark of Bloomsbury Publishing Plc

First published 2013

British Library Cataloguing-in-Publication Data
A catalogue record for this book is available from the British Library.

ISBN: HB: 978-0-8578-5682-1
         PB: 978-0-8578-5772-9
      ePDF: 978-0-8578-5790-3
      ePub: 978-1-4725-1725-8

Library of Congress Cataloging-in-Publication Data

Prototype : design and craft in the 21st century / edited by Louise Valentine.
    pages cm
  Includes bibliographical references and index.
    ISBN 978-0-85785-772-9 (pbk.) — ISBN 978-0-85785-682-1 (hardback) —
ISBN 978-0-85785-790-3 (epdf) — ISBN 978-1-4725-1725-8 (epub)
  1. Prototypes, Engineering.   I. Valentine, Louise.
  TS171.8.P76 2013
  620'.0042—dc23

                    2013039560

Typeset by Apex CoVantage, LLC

CONTENTS

LIST OF ILLUSTRATIONS AND TABLES

FIGURES

TABLES

EDITOR'S NOTE

The book seeks to capture the spirit of a symposium entitled 'Prototype: Craft in the Future Tense'. By design and through research, I lead a team who brought together a broad range of speakers, including artists, designers, engineers, historians, musicians, theoreticians and scientists. The research-led event was made possible through the contributions of nineteen international professionals. Most of the essays selected for this volume were originally delivered as invited papers at 'Prototype: Craft in the Future Tense' held at the University of Dundee, Scotland, 10–11 June 2010. The papers have since undergone revision.

Louise Valentine

ACKNOWLEDGEMENTS

Prototype is the result of an Arts and Humanities Research Council, UK-funded study entitled, 'Craft as a Form of Mindful Inquiry'. In creating this book, I would like to thank the authors who have taken great care and time to reflect and share their knowledge and ideas in writing with us.

I would also like to thank Rebecca Barden, Abbie Sharman, Sheri Sipka, Simon Longman, Simon Cowell and the team at Bloomsbury Publishing for guiding me through the book-writing process.

The support and encouragement of many colleagues over the past three years has been magical. In particular, a great deal of thanks is due to Seaton Baxter and Fraser Bruce for their steadfast collegiality and trust, to Sean Kingsley and Cathy Brown for helping to organize the successful event, and in doing so, preparing the basis for this book, to Kathleen Brown for her calm manner and meticulous attention to detail in the copy-editing process, to Paula Francis for her exquisite administrative support in all of our academic research endeavours, to Frances Stevenson, Jennifer Ballie, Joanna Bletcher, Saskia Coulson, Sarah Cox, Lisa Cresswell and Rebecca Lindsay for their inquiring minds and resolute courage in the pursuit of new knowledge, and to Creative Scotland, Duncan of Jordanstone College of Art and Design, University of Dundee and the Arts and Humanities Research Council for their financial support.

Finally, my deepest and most precious thank you goes to my family for teaching me every day to imagine and believe.

Louise Valentine

PREFACE

It was a warm, bright and sunny afternoon in Dundee, Scotland, when this book was born. Warm *and* sunny days are not all that common in that part of the world, so perhaps it seemed doubly auspicious. I was visiting from London to co-convene a symposium on the idea of the prototype with Louise Valentine and also to see the town. As the future home of the Victoria and Albert Museum's (V&A) first regional affiliate, Dundee has a particular importance for us at the museum. V&A at Dundee will be many things: an impressive building designed by architect Kengo Kuma, a major contribution to Scotland's creative economy and an ideal platform in which to present design of the past and present. Given all that awaited, it is no surprise that the future was on my mind. On that day, in fact, I conceived the idea of a major exhibition about the way that artists and designers have envisioned things to come. Provisionally entitled *The Future: A History*, that project will come to fruition in 2017. It will include projective and divinatory objects from all around the world, presenting the full range of the V&A's collections in future tense.

Within this exhibition, the prototype will have a special place. It is, perhaps, the quintessential future-facing object. Fundamentally, design is an act of the imagination, not entirely distinct from art, fiction or even night-time dreams. Like these other areas of unbridled human creativity, design trades in images, storylines and flashes of insight. But it is different in one key respect. In most cases, design is conducted under extreme practical pressure. It must be optimized according to a whole range of variables. All the more so if the design is intended for mass production, in which case, it may have a large economic footprint. This exposes the designer to all the attendant concerns of big business: sustainability, unit cost, financial risk, health and safety regulations and brand management. This is quite a lot of responsibility for one product to bear; the prototype is the means by which that pressure is negotiated.

The prototype acts as both a proving ground and a point of reference for the rest of the design process. All the lines of force that bear in on the designer converge, in turn, upon the prototype. It must materialize the possible while also conforming to the limits of the job. The prototype reflects a myriad of concerns, from the purely aesthetic to the straightforwardly functional. It embodies the peculiar character of design, which more than any other creative discipline finds its inspiration in constraint.

For a designer, a prototype is first and foremost a conceptual object—a means of ideation rather than production. Yet it is supremely physical. It must be made from materials, using tools, and these will be key factors affecting the design. If you model a car in sculpted clay, folded paper or three-dimensional rendering software, you are bound to get very different results.

A prototype is also a great way to start a conversation. In discussions between a designer and a client, a user, a manufacturer or another designer, even a very simple prop can be worth more than any number of words. This is not to say, however, that it is a truth machine. Prototypes can be beautiful lies, promising something that cannot (or will not) be delivered. The skilful designer knows how to use that rhetoric to advantage.

Of course, not all prototypes are physical things. They can also be processes, networks, technologies. Anything in its test phase, really, is a kind of prototype. We might, indeed, want to speak of an activity—prototyping—rather than a class of object. What kind of activity is this? Again, there is no one answer. Prototyping can be a profession—as in pattern cutting, architectural modelling and engineering. It can also be a system, or rather a conjoined system of systems, each called into being for a specific purpose. Consider the number and variety of preparatory stages involved in the creation of a single smartphone. Few people outside the worlds of design, research and development, and manufacturing ever see prototypes. Yet their influence is all around us.

Just as I thought of an exhibition on that day in Dundee, my co-convenor conceived a book. That future, anyway, has come to pass, for you are reading it now. Like our symposium (from which many of the contributors were selected), the volume includes a range of voices on the topic, nearly as varied as prototypes themselves. There are designers who view the prototype as a medium of problem-solving, expression and exploration. There are also makers. One might say that prototypes inhabit the middle ground between those two notoriously slippery terms, craft and design; even in today's world of three-dimensional printing and digital rendering, most prototypes are made by hand. They represent the artisanal dimension of the design process. In this book, you will also find historians who view the prototype as evidence—an unusually direct way of accessing past intentions, which may have been worn smooth and undetectable through a process of later development. And then there are medical researchers, psychologists, technologists and even a space architect, all of whom focus on the utility of a prototype in discursive and research-intensive contexts.

Louise Valentine is an ideal editor to bring all these voices into some kind of harmony; an industrial design specialist by training, her interest in prototyping and craft includes the creation of ideas, meaning and forms, not just the processes of the workshop. No volume could hope to provide a comprehensive account of this multivalent and infinitely fluid topic, but with the help of her contributors, Louise has made remarkable inroads. This book provides routes into the subject and out again, tools for thinking, case studies and provocations. How like a prototype: all the key issues have been considered, yet so much is left to be done.

Glenn Adamson

CONTRIBUTORS

*Speaker at 'Prototype: Craft in the Future Tense' symposium, University of Dundee, 2010.

Constance Adams is a specialist in high-performance architecture and design innovation, particularly in the area of architecture for human spaceflight. Currently leading research for Synthesis LLP, her work for NASA has included performing operations integration for the International Space Station, crew systems design and new module architecture. Adams's tenure as architectural consultant to NASA and to commercial space ventures has sensitized her to issues of human–machine interface, sustainable systems, the importance of biomimetic design and the need for new ways of addressing risk in the design and building professions. Adams translated an early specialization in urban design and institutional architecture into a unique portfolio of designs for NASA's human spaceflight programme, including two surface habitats for lunar/Mars exploration, a long-duration crew transit spacecraft, and vehicle architecture for the X-38 Crew Return Vehicle, the larger Crew Transfer Vehicle and the Orbital Space Plane. She is one of the principal designers who took part in the winning design for the Virgin Galactic hangar facility at New Mexico's Spaceport America. This work has been published in *Metropolis*, *ID*, *Wired*, *Popular Science*, *Architectural Record*, *Newsweek* and other journals and has been exhibited at the Art Institute of Chicago and the Yale School of Architecture. She has won several NASA awards for her innovative technologies.

Glenn Adamson leads the Research Department's activities at the Victoria and Albert Museum (V&A) in London, working closely with colleagues within the museum and in collaboration with scholars and institutions worldwide. He holds a PhD in Art History from Yale University and was previously curator at the Chipstone Foundation in Milwaukee. Dr Adamson cocurated (with Jane Pavitt) the exhibition 'Postmodernism: Style and Subversion, 1970 to 1990', which opened at the V&A in 2011. He has also written widely on craft history and theory in such books as *Thinking Through Craft* (2007), *The Craft Reader*

(2010) and *The Invention of Craft* (2013); he has edited numerous publications, including the triannual *Journal of Modern Craft*, the volume *Global Design History* (co-edited with Giorgio Riello and Sarah Teasley, 2011) and *Surface Tensions* (co-edited with Victoria Kelley, 2012).

Seaton Baxter has academic qualifications in building technology and philosophy. He worked for twenty years in agricultural research mainly concerned with the design of buildings and equipment for animal welfare before joining the Robert Gordon University, Aberdeen, in 1983 as head of the School of Construction Management, Property and Surveying. At the Robert Gordon University, he acted as assistant principal, dean and reader, where he established the Centre for Environmental Studies (c. 1994) and the first ever MSc in Ecological Design. He is currently an honorary professor at Dundee University where he heads the Centre for the Study of Natural Design. Seaton has worked with several Scottish environmental nongovernmental organizations (NGOs), including the Scottish Environment Link, Association for the Protection of Rural Scotland, and Deeside Forest Advisory Group, and he was formerly a board member of Scottish Natural Heritage. He was awarded an OBE by the Queen for his services to Scotland's Natural Heritage in 1998.

*Stuart I. Brown is team leader of Professor Sir Alfred Cuschieri's Surgical Technology Group, a Research and Development team based at the University of Dundee's Institute for Medical Science and Technology. One of the Group's central remits is to produce novel devices in support of efforts by leading clinicians to pioneer new surgical procedures. Nearly all the Group's work is concerned with Minimal Access Surgery (MAS), popularly known as keyhole surgery and, in particular, new approaches which aim to reduce the number of keyholes from four or five to just one.

Fraser Bruce investigates how organizations can use design-thinking and ecological-thinking as strategic tools in order to gain competitive advantage. He began his career in the early 1990s in laser manufacturing before becoming a mechanical engineer developing, as part of a team, novel instruments, manipulators and new optical techniques for laparoscopic surgery. In 1999 he progressed in product development engineering, focusing on an Excellence Programme for Small and Medium-sized Enterprises. In 2003 Fraser made the transition from industry to academia where he now teaches strategy, innovation, prototyping, design and ecological thinking to undergraduates, graduates and doctoral researchers.

*Rosan Chow is visiting professor of Designwissenschaft at the Muthesius Academy of Fine Arts and Design in Kiel, Germany. She holds a BA and an MDes in Visual Communication Design from the University of Alberta, Canada and a PhD in Designwissenschaft from the University of Arts Braunschweig, Germany. Her research and teaching focus on the fundamentals of design. Based on this knowledge, she develops methods and tools aiming to advance design practice and education. With Professor Wolfgang Jonas, she has also developed a design process tool called MAPS.

Steve Gill is a product designer with twenty years of experience in industry and a professor of interactive product design for the Cardiff School of Art & Design, Wales. He has designed or managed around fifty products to market and has published widely. He is currently cowriting a book on physicality with Professor Alan Dix of the University of Lancaster, UK called *Touch IT*.

*Catharine Rossi is a senior lecturer in design history in the School of Art and Design History at Kingston University, London. In 2011 she completed an Arts and Humanities Research Council (AHRC) Collaborative Doctoral Award in 'Modern Craft: History, Theory and Practice' in the RCA/V&A History of Design Department with a thesis entitled 'Crafting Design in Italy, from Post-war to Postmodernism' that will be published by Manchester University Press in 2014. Research areas include twentieth- and twenty-first-century craft and design, with a particular interest in postwar Italy. Publications include articles in *Design and Culture*, *The Journal of Design History* and *The Journal of Modern Craft* and a chapter on Memphis in the V&A exhibition catalogue *Postmodernism: Style & Subversion 1970–1990*.

*Elizabeth B.-N. Sanders joined the Design Department at The Ohio State University as an associate professor in 2011 after having worked as a design research consultant in industry since 1981. She has practised participatory design research within and between all the design disciplines. Her research today focuses on participatory design research, collective creativity and transdisciplinarity. Her goal is to bring participatory, human-centred design thinking and cocreation practices to the challenges we face for the future. Liz has a PhD in Experimental and Quantitative Psychology and a BA in both Psychology and Anthropology.

*Michael Schrage is a Fellow with the Massachusetts Institute of Technology (MIT) Sloan School's Center for Digital Business and a senior advisor to MIT's

Security Studies Program. He previously held the position of codirector of the Media Lab E-Markets Initiative at MIT. He advises organizations on the economics of innovation through rapid experimentation, simulation and digital design. His research and advisory work explores the role of models, prototypes and simulations as collaborative media for managing innovation risk. His ongoing work on strategic and 'just in time' experimentation is at the core of several corporate transformation efforts. He has been an advisor/consultant to such organizations as Accenture, Google, Siemens, Wells Fargo, Microsoft, PwC, British Telecom, BP, Mars and NASDAQ. He performs nonclassified work for the National Security Council, DARPA and the Pentagon's Office of Net Assessment on command, control and cyber-conflict management issues. He also helped set up the MIT/CSIS workshops on the design, acquisition and procurement of complex systems. He is the author of two books: *Serious Play: How the World's Best Companies Simulate to Innovate* and *Shared Minds—The New Technologies of Collaboration*.

*Frederic J. Schwartz is a professor, teaching the history of art and architecture at University College London. He has lectured and published widely on modern architecture and design, the critical theory of the Frankfurt School, the German avant-garde of the early twentieth century and the history of art as an academic discipline. He has also been an editor of the *Oxford Art Journal* since 1996. He is the author of *The Werkbund: Design Theory and Mass Culture* (1996, German edn 1999) and *Blind Spots: Critical Theory and the History of Art in Twentieth-Century Germany* (2005), and he has written extensively on the Bauhaus, twentieth-century German architecture and the Frankfurt School Critical Theory.

*Pieter Jan Stappers made the switch to industrial design engineering at TU Delft after an education in experimental physics (MSc 1984), and he followed a research path which led from human perception, spatial imagery and virtual reality (PhD in 1992) to design tools and participatory design techniques. As full professor of design techniques within the innovative ID-StudioLab, renowned for its high-quality design research (http://www.studiolab.nl/), he leads a group of researchers and educators that focus on the early phases of design, including mapping user contexts and exploring understanding through prototypes.

Louise Valentine is a senior lecturer in design and craft at the University of Dundee in Scotland. She studied industrial design before gaining her doctoral degree in 2004 entitled 'The Activity of Rhetoric within the Process of a Designer's Thinking'. Her research focuses on design and craft mindfulness. It focuses on how we perceive design as a process and the means with which to employ designer's capacities and capabilities to analyse performance across a range of scenarios. She is editor of *Past, Present and Future Craft Practice* and a member of the team for the £45m Victoria and Albert Museum (V&A) at Dundee initiative, which will be an international centre for design housed in a world-class building designed by the Japanese architectural firm Kengo Kuma and Associates. She is a Fellow of the Royal Society of the Arts.

*Hazel White** was a design and craft practitioner in the 'Craft as a Form of Mindful Inquiry' study within the major Arts and Humanities Research Council project, 'Past, Present and Future Craft Practice' (2007–2010), commissioned for her collaborative approach to making with multimedia artists, computer programmers and designers. She is director of the Master of Design for Services Programme at the University of Dundee, UK. Her recent research, design and consultancy include work for National Health Service Scotland and the Scottish Government, The Children's Hospice Association Scotland (CHAS) and the Chartered Institute for Public Finance Accountancy.

INTRODUCTION

LOUISE VALENTINE

Prototype describes a project that has been carried out as part of the *Craft as a Form of Mindful Inquiry* postdoctoral study. It describes the future focus element of this research where a step-change for craft education and discourse was proposed.

This introductory chapter offers a framework for the ideas within the book. It starts with a brief overview of the research aims and methodology of *Craft as a Form of Mindful Inquiry*. It progresses to the rationale for focusing on prototype as a strategic tool, doing so through insights gleaned from a qualitative study of five leading British craft practitioners (Valentine 2010, 2011). The approach to sequencing of the chapters is presented and followed by a summary of each invited author's contribution. The conclusion articulates the intention behind *Prototype*.

CRAFT AS A FORM OF MINDFUL INQUIRY

Craft as a Form of Mindful Inquiry is an academic research project funded through the Art and Humanities Research Council, one of seven academic research councils in the UK. The five-year project set out to evaluate the aesthetics embodied in craft by studying methodologies rooted in historical and contemporary practice (2005–10)[1]. The study places practitioners and their visual thinking at the centre of investigation. It seeks knowledge of craft from a strategic perspective and asks how the sector can regenerate itself.

Mindful Inquiry is the methodological framework for investigating historical and contemporary designers' practice and for understanding future notions of craft practice. It is a philosophy of research and a synthesis of four traditions: critical social theory, phenomenology, hermeneutics and Buddhism (Bentz and Shapiro 1998). At the heart of the approach is mindfulness, which is a concern for living or being in the present moment, an ability to become aware of the assumptions hindering our progress and the impact these illusions have on our thoughts, ideas and relationships (Figures 0.1–0.4). It attends to change and perpetual activity within both the research context and the subject under investigation. It places the human condition at the centre of investigation.

Drawing on the words of Jon Kabat-Zinn (1994), the approach can be understood as follows:

> The spirit of inquiry is fundamental to living mindfully. Inquiry is not just a way to solve problems. It is a way to make sure you are staying in touch with the basic mystery that is life itself and of our presence in it . . . Inquiry doesn't mean looking for answers, especially quick answers which come out of superficial thinking. It means asking without expecting answers, just pondering the questions, carrying the wondering with you, letting it percolate, bubble, cook, ripen, come in and out of awareness, just as everything else comes in and out of awareness. Inquiry is not so much thinking about answers, although the questioning will produce a lot of thinking that looks like answers. It really involves just listening to the thinking that your questioning invokes, as if you were sitting by the side of the stream of your own thoughts, listening to the water flow over and around the rocks, listening, listening and watching an occasional leaf or twig as it is carried along. (Kabat-Zinn cited in Bentz and Shapiro 1998: 39)

A designer's craft practice is an interrelated system of activities informed by the everyday and the unusual: a continuous, organic process with embedded layers of meaning and experience. It can be a highly sociable and emotional journey involving a wide range of influences, such as people, places, personality and personal capabilities (Valentine 2004). As such, the philosophy of mindfulness chimes with designers of craft—ceramic, glass, jewellery and textile, for example—as it reflects the traditionally slow, independent and contemplative values underpinning their creativity.

For me, craft as a process is comprised of many layers, which run concurrently throughout the life of a maker, and each activity can be considered a creative discourse with its own pathway and conditions. As such, the craft process is best understood by observing practice over a series of years rather than through the creation of an individual product created in a short period. This is because time allows for maturation of ideas and a deepened understanding of self, which are reciprocal: two primary and intertwined acts contributing to visual integrity, which brings a sense of well-being (or vice versa), which is a central aspiration of the maker (Valentine 2011).

Phenomenology is part of Mindful Inquiry. It is very useful for noticing what things we take for granted, encouraging us to see things in a new way, to step

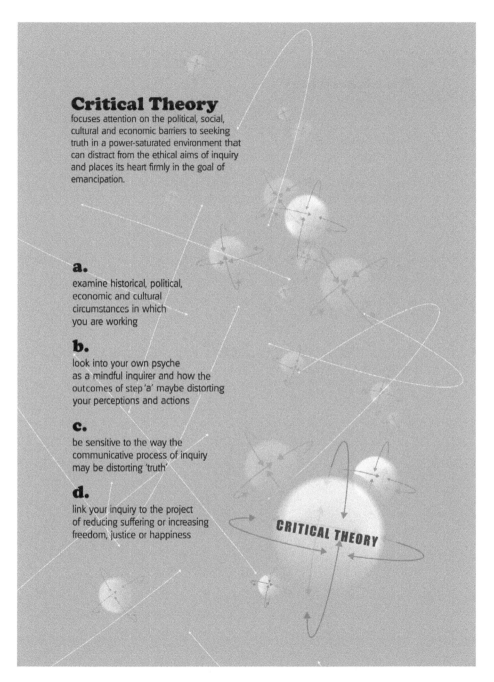

Critical Theory focuses attention on the political, social, cultural and economic barriers to seeking truth in a power-saturated environment that can distract from the ethical aims of inquiry and places its heart firmly in the goal of emancipation.

a.
examine historical, political, economic and cultural circumstances in which you are working

b.
look into your own psyche as a mindful inquirer and how the outcomes of step 'a' maybe distorting your perceptions and actions

c.
be sensitive to the way the communicative process of inquiry may be distorting 'truth'

d.
link your inquiry to the project of reducing suffering or increasing freedom, justice or happiness

CRITICAL THEORY

Figure 0.1   Valentine's infographic presents Critical Theory as one component in a three-dimensional inter-related system, which is mediated through time. Critical Theory is one of four traditions within Mindful Inquiry. It has four lines of investigation (a–d) which are dynamically related and result in a rhetorical relationship. © Louise Valentine.

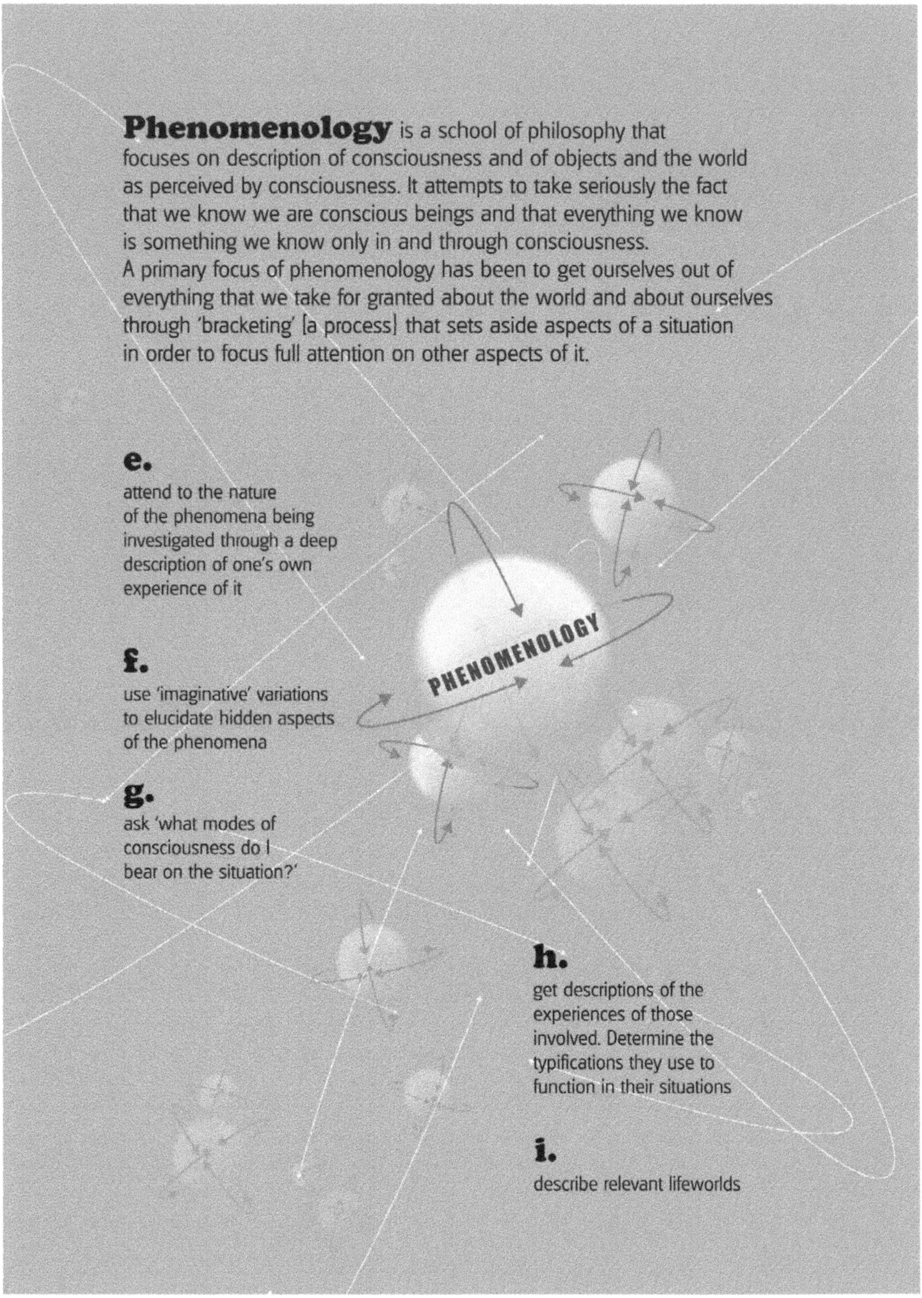

Phenomenology is a school of philosophy that focuses on description of consciousness and of objects and the world as perceived by consciousness. It attempts to take seriously the fact that we know we are conscious beings and that everything we know is something we know only in and through consciousness. A primary focus of phenomenology has been to get ourselves out of everything that we take for granted about the world and about ourselves through 'bracketing' [a process] that sets aside aspects of a situation in order to focus full attention on other aspects of it.

e.
attend to the nature of the phenomena being investigated through a deep description of one's own experience of it

f.
use 'imaginative' variations to elucidate hidden aspects of the phenomena

g.
ask 'what modes of consciousness do I bear on the situation?'

PHENOMENOLOGY

h.
get descriptions of the experiences of those involved. Determine the typifications they use to function in their situations

i.
describe relevant lifeworlds

Figure 0.2   Phenomenology is the second of four traditions within Mindful Inquiry. The infographic seeks to communicate the dynamic environment in which decision-making occurs through the practice of Mindful Inquiry, resulting in a nonlinear process. Phenomenology has five critical reflective steps in its process (e–i). © Louise Valentine.

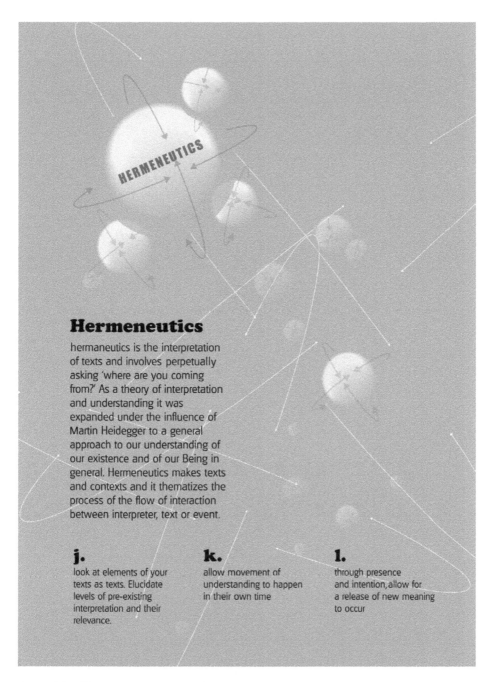

Hermeneutics

hermaneutics is the interpretation of texts and involves perpetually asking 'where are you coming from?' As a theory of interpretation and understanding it was expanded under the influence of Martin Heidegger to a general approach to our understanding of our existence and of our Being in general. Hermeneutics makes texts and contexts and it thematizes the process of the flow of interaction between interpreter, text or event.

j.
look at elements of your texts as texts. Elucidate levels of pre-existing interpretation and their relevance.

k.
allow movement of understanding to happen in their own time

l.
through presence and intention, allow for a release of new meaning to occur

Figure 0.3   Hermeneutics is the third research tradition within Mindful Inquiry. In viewing the methodology as a dynamic system, the issues of 'time' and 'change' are brought into focus with mindfulness, or being in the present moment, of critical importance. Hermeneutics has three steps within its process (j–l). © Louise Valentine.

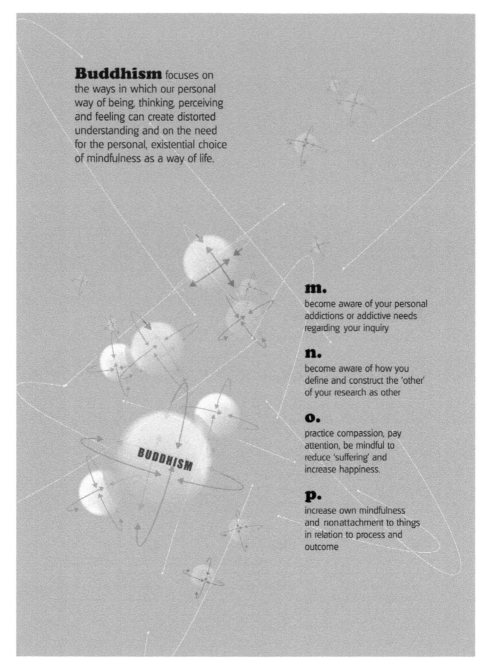

Buddhism focuses on the ways in which our personal way of being, thinking, perceiving and feeling can create distorted understanding and on the need for the personal, existential choice of mindfulness as a way of life.

m.
become aware of your personal addictions or addictive needs regarding your inquiry

n.
become aware of how you define and construct the 'other' of your research as other

o.
practice compassion, pay attention, be mindful to reduce 'suffering' and increase happiness.

p.
increase own mindfulness and nonattachment to things in relation to process and outcome

BUDDHISM

Figure 0.4   Buddhism is the fourth tradition within Mindful Inquiry. It has four steps within its process (m–p). It embodies the personal engagement and multiple ways in which the four-part journey can be experienced. © Louise Valentine.

outside of our culture and question our habitual ways of describing and defining things (Bentz and Shapiro 1998). A phenomenological perspective endeavours to break with inherited understandings in order to awaken fresh experience of a phenomena (Crotty 1998). As Alvesson and Sköldberg say, 'Experience itself becomes the point of departure' (2009: 76). In this respect, it is part of mindfulness. In a world where the concept of 'change' is a given and technological progress pervades our everyday existence, this viewpoint supports the questioning of basic assumptions about the concept of 'making' craft, a reappraisal of how we discuss it and the development of innovation in it.

In working with over fifty international design and craft practitioners (2005–9) in this study, a paradox was noted in that there is an eclectic mix of influences within individuals' creative processes, yet the diversity of influences largely disappears within academically devised discourses for craft; they can appear closed. For example, in creative practice, a conceptual jeweller can draw on knowledge of culture, human-computer interaction, craft, critical design, English literature and ethnography. A pliquc-à-jour cnameller can draw on science fiction, botany, craft and design history. A metalwork designer can draw on knowledge from science, mathematics, sport and design education. In academe, however, the popular model is for a diverse and international group of artists, crafters, designers and (at times) curators to look at their respective history, theory and practice solely from within their own particular perspectives. Without undermining the value of this approach, it arguably removes the inherent pluralism and cultural diversity within the life of 'making'. Yet, if innovation is a central issue for designers and craft practice, incorporating pluralism and cultural diversity into strategic discourse should occur. For example, conversation between people who would not traditionally be in conversation with one another—such as one of us in conversation with a world-renowned space architect, who imagines long-term futures, and through our discussion, the architect encourages us to imagine the consequences of our actions in a 100-year time frame. Or imagine us in conversation with a management guru, who redefines how we think about innovation, or a pioneering designer, who challenges the environments in which design is taught, or a historian, who suggests how we can learn from past theories and philosophies to critique our ideas when considering the future.

Coupled with this perceived need for change in how we communicate craft is the transformation in global circumstance. We live in unanticipated times. A major feature of the emergent and unfamiliar scenarios of today is that they are extremely complex, requiring radical thinking and intense transdisciplinary collaborations for their solution (Brown 2008; Peat 2008). Aligned to this global change is what strategic design researcher Tom Inns refers to as an 'explosion of interest' in design thinking (2010: 21). Design's value has transformed globally in the twenty-first century, and its significance for resolving highly complex problems is more widely understood and debated (Borja de Mozota 2006; Brown 2009; Buchanan, Doordan and Margolin 2010; Evans 2011; Fry 2009; Inns, Baxter and Murphy 2006; Jahnke 2012; Kimbell 2011; Krippendorf 2006; Redström 2006; Stickdorn and Schneider 2011).

So, with a concern for increased innovation in craft and an increasing complexity and growing use of interdisciplinary teams to resolve emergent problems, it is perhaps of no surprise that the idea of a theme is selected to unify a divergent group of thinkers. Or, that prototype is the selected theme. This is because the purpose of a prototype remains constant, irrespective of its form and aesthetic: it is a language, process and tool for progressing ideas towards a useful end goal. The prototype is an existing and integral aspect of both design and craft. It is also a concept recognized outside of design and craft as an object conceived as a means to an end beyond itself—a way of envisioning the future.

PROTOTYPE: DESIGN AND CRAFT

The term design and craft is beguiling—an idiom hinting at a world filled with creativity and imagination, yet simultaneously, it is a phrase bereft of meaning. Historically, the two fields of design and craft have experienced multiple cycles of intimacy and distance with variable levels of friendship and respect. It is a deeply rhetorical relationship where the need to understand each other results in a perpetual open-ended conversation. It is a dialogue guided by external forces, such as industrialization, ethics, socioeconomic politics and science. Underpinning both practices is the conception and planning of ideas where imagination and the ability to envision is core: a concern for the integration of technical, material and aesthetic issues existing within a social, cultural and philosophical framework.

Materiality combines the two. It also defines them as distinctly individual. At first glance, this appears contradictory, yet close inspection of the values underpinning their independent construction details why materiality is both glue and solvent. As a dissolving substance, it appears in the form of design and craft's alternative approaches to manufacturing. In a crude delineation of their values, using a traditional industrial setting, the production of design is most often directed by the mantra 'high volume + fast delivery = lower cost + repeat business', whereas craft's ethos is 'low volume + slow delivery = mid-to-high cost + repeat business'. As a consequence, the commercial markets and audiences determine whether design and craft have a relation at all. Yet, as we embrace the second decade of the twenty-first century, the commercial viability of design and craft lies as much with their strategic capabilities as it does their operational preferences towards new product design and development. Here, we shift our gaze from understanding the value of design and craft as personified objects to the behaviours and psyche underpinning their thinking processes. In this context, materiality acts as an adhesive or bonding mechanism and manifests itself via prototypes and prototyping, where the act of critically questioning the mind's eye is achieved through the physical creation of an idea or series of ideas.

Prototyping is a key means with which an individual's imagination is tenaciously explored, tested, broken and rebuilt—pushed and pulled into some kind of order, if for only a fleeting moment. It is a conscious escape from reality, and at its best, it is an uncontrolled extravaganza of the mind with scant regard for conventional wisdom. That is not to say the process is mindless, simply that it cannot and should not be bound by certainty. The prototype is the friend we turn to when we are unsure, the compass when we are lost and the ally who comes to our aid when we are in trouble. She is the nurse who soothes our ailments and nurtures our well-being. As a teacher, she helps us to listen intently and see our mistakes, encouraging us to work through the difficulties and to achieve our best. Her capacity to bring out the most playful side of our nature is inspirational, and when we fail to face our responsibilities, her reprimanding is respected. Through time the prototype has proven to be design and craft's most loyal and trustworthy compatriot. Yet, she is often in the shadows of our lives, acknowledged and at times praised for her strength and support, but rarely, if ever, invited to take centre stage. A consummate parent to her children one might say.

This notion of the prototype as parent is an unusual perspective. Traditionally, the prototype is viewed as subordinate, the child of design or craft. The conventional approach to discussing prototypes and prototyping is with a concern for the iteration of an idea and the effective management of risk-taking, and as a consequence, failure and success. Typically, it is about the process of research and development in a product or market-specific context; the subject asks questions such as 'what does it [the idea] look like', 'how does it operate', 'does it meet customer requirements and expectations' and 'how might it be improved'. In design and craft, the role of prototypes is most commonly discussed in product and service development processes, regularly cited as a method for nurturing innovation within the process of problem solving.

A second convention is to contain a discussion of the prototype within one area of expertise. For example, in manufacturing, where discussion is most often contained to delineating between traditional methods of manufacturing, such as turning, milling and casting, with modern digital fabrication methods, such as rapid prototyping.

Serious play is a core tenet of Mindful Inquiry (Bentz and Shapiro 1998). In this respect, it is once again akin to design and craft practice in that it is a theory employed (often through prototyping) to uncover blind spots and expose weaknesses and limitations in an individual's positioning when conceiving and creating ideas (Brown 2009; Dunne 2005; Koskinen, Zimmerman, Binder, Redström and Wensveen, 2011; Schrage 2000; Ulrich and Eppinger, 2003). Here, it is employed to acknowledge the tradition of prototyping in design and craft, but more importantly, to invert the conventional perspective of seeing prototype as a secondary subject of discussion and elevate it to a primary position. The intention is to draw on a range of expertise on the value of the prototype as a generic problem solving approach to navigating change. This viewpoint is unconventional, but given the exigency to rethink how we do things, it is arguably a necessary perspective to consider. It also reflects the growing interest in cocreation and collaboration because they are growing characteristics of the interconnected world in which we live.

As in life, it is people who are the most important part of prototyping, design and craft. We choose to invite people into our lives, and we choose to accept people who have fallen serendipitously into our lives. The relationships we neglect and nurture ultimately inform our perspective and judgements. In the following discourse, contributions are culturally diverse and have been brought together from pioneers in the fields of space architecture, management and design and leading world experts of craft, design, ecology, history and medical engineering.

CHAPTER SEQUENCING AND SUMMARIES

The voices in this prototype are geographically and culturally diverse, with American, British and European perspectives on offer from seven knowledge domains. Reflected in this are also four approaches to discussing the prototype: (*a*) theory, (*b*) theory with supporting case material evidencing the theory in practice, (*c*) practice and (*d*) practice with supporting reference to theoretical framework(s). To support this content, the book's chapter sequence moves from 'what is' into 'how to' and vice versa, incorporating independent reflections and shared activities surrounding prototype: design and craft.

The prominent MIT media and business theorist Michael Schrage offers a theory of innovation based on the idea of 'serious play'. In the opening chapter 'Crafting Interactions: The Purpose and Practice of Serious Play', Schrage focuses on identifying the fundamental principles of the craft and culture of prototyping. He argues that the craft of prototyping is best understood in the context of three interrelated principles: hypotheses, marketplaces and playgrounds. Here, the prototype is best seen as a nonprecious object, an opportunity to explore failure and be deeply imaginative, where emphasis is given to the act of developing an idea and asking questions of its value rather than the act of showing a developed idea and telling its value. He suggests the 'charismodel'—a type of prototype that exudes charisma and is extraordinarily motivational and inspirational to a wide range of people. Why is this important? Because they induce overachievement by others, 'Just as charismatic athletes lift the level of play, charismatic prototypes elevate the quality of creativity'.

In Chapter 2, British design historian Catharine Rossi offers a richly researched account of Italian prototyping practices, ranging from industrial concerns (Olivetti and Alessi) to the radical design groups Global Tools, Studio Alchimia and Memphis. In 'From Mari to Memphis: The Role of Prototypes in Italian Radical and Postmodern Design', Rossi posits that within the copious writings about Memphis—its impact on design and interpretations of design—there is a missing discourse: understanding the work as 'one-off handcrafted prototypes'. She believes this situation can be understood by studying the role of the prototype in three distinct periods of change: the early postwar period of 1945–60, the mid-1960s and the late 1970s to early 1980s. Rossi articulates the impact of this transformation by noting a shift in emphasis in design by designers from design as product to design as process, so much so that by the 1970s 'the connection between prototype and product [loosened]'; the boundary was fuzzy and increased in fuzziness for most of the decade, negatively impacting its relation with the marketplace in terms of retailing. The argument closes by attending to the early 1980s, particularly the Memphis group, who renegotiated the relation between artisan-designer-investor and patron-manufacturer-audience.

In Chapter 3, the engineer Fraser Bruce and ecological theoretician Seaton Baxter examine the world in which we live as a series of multiple crises, which appear to have culminated in one large, integrated, turbulent emergency verging on chaos. A major feature of these new problems is that there is no precedent to learn from; the issues are seriously complex and require serious imagining and transdisciplinary teamwork for their solution. They consider prototyping in the context of problem-solving, and they argue for a new category of problem to be understood by designers—one that centres on living systems, retains the large-scale, interconnected web of living systems and deeply considers the consequences of individual actions, namely, Alien Problems. Alien Problems can only be achieved once the social and operational problems of alien team-working are understood as symptoms of the problem. These symptoms must be addressed as part of a holistic approach to Alien Problem–solving. In drawing a conclusion, fifteen insights surrounding Alien Problems are combined from all three of the 'serious imagining' experiments spanning a thirty-year period.

In Chapter 4, leading industrial designer Elizabeth Sanders invites us to reconsider the prototype as a way of making sense of the future. Here, the prototype is not simply an object indicating the potential form and function of a subsequent product; it is a tool that re-enters the design process at several stages, each time taking on a different role in relation to time and space. In 'Prototyping for the Design Spaces of the Future', Sanders focuses the discussion on the context and subject of 'change' in design over the last thirty years. She observes four 'manifestations', or signs, of adjustment and articulates how they have revealed an exigency for new approaches, languages, mindsets and tools by designers and design researchers. In response to these emerging design spaces, Sanders offers the Participatory Prototyping Cycle: a cocreation tool and language for the new landscape of design in action, where designers are attending to larger and more complex situations than before. Sanders believes we need to consider the implications of globally shifting landscapes on design education and the impact of emerging design spaces on future curricula.

British artist and interactive jeweller Hazel White provides a focused discussion of open-ended prototypes as a means of working with rural communities. In her chapter 'Handle with Care', White invites us to imagine a world in which material and personal resonance are central to the development of sociodigital design within culturally specific context(s). From the perspective of an interactive jeweller and through her project *Hamefarer's Kist* (set in the Scottish Shetland Isles, 2010), she offers insight into Anthony Dunne's concept of the 'genotype'. White argues for the relevance of genotyping as an alternative to prototyping for craft contemporary practice, offering a method which focuses on the ability to develop new ideas. She describes the concept and process of realizing the *Hamefarer's Kist*, which 'is a suggestion of how older people in care homes could share experiences with [geographically] distant relatives'. It is concerned with embedding memory in objects through interactive technology in order to support the well-being of elderly people.

Pieter Jan Stappers, a Dutch designer and researcher from ID StudioLab at TU Delft in the Netherlands, discusses the pedagogical role of prototyping in the vividly innovative context of universities like that of Delft. He argues that making prototypes is a key part of developing knowledge and developing questions for critically analysing knowledge. Stappers presents the prototype as a conceptual and technical structure that 'confronts the world', suggesting we are in a period when products themselves are taking on the provisional qualities of prototypes. In his chapter 'Prototypes as a Central Vein for Knowledge Development',

Stappers argues that prototyping generates and facilitates the communication of knowledge within and between research projects. He also advocates that prototypes are vehicles for maintaining a relation between theory and practice in research for design, suggesting this tenet has been largely undervalued. The intention of the chapter is to share five insights about the value of prototypes for innovation, learned through twenty years of design research.

In the next chapter, 'Techne and Logos at the Edge of Space', pioneering Space Architect Constance Adams shares insights into the conceptual and practical aspects of aerospace design and its associated challenges, be they intellectual, material, technical and/or technological. She talks about the mission to Mars and high-tech versus low-tech prototyping, and presents the relation between concept, construction and actual use in the development of new space-ready products. With regard to prototyping, Adams believes, 'there is no substitute for the human hand'. She acknowledges the contradictions inherent within future design for spacecraft journeys and the reality of finding a solution while concurrently generating a new problem, as this work is often on a scale and in a time frame rarely considered by human beings. Her underlying message is that design and craft practitioners need to take greater responsibility in their strategic decision-making processes, and she advocates that we consider doing so in the context of a 100-year time frame—not that it will provide answers, but it will encourage us to take deep responsibility for the long-term implications of our actions.

'Prototopia: Craft, Type and Utopia in Historical Perspective' by Frederic Schwartz, an historian of art, architecture and a particular form of critical thought, offers a complex discourse concerned with the concept of the prototype as a 'logical and temporal conundrum' and how thinking through this can help 'thinking in general'. At the heart of Schwartz's analysis is the struggle between the utopian impulse of craft 'in the future tense' and the various historical 'realities' which at first glance appear to bring craft back to the past. His journey takes us through modes of production, habits of consumption, changes in the sense of time, utopias, ontologies, ornament, design, type or category of form, logic, physicality, politics and bricolage: at all times, he gathers together these individual elements to produce a process of thinking that embraces and supports complexity rather than produce a cohesive whole.

Distinguished medical engineer Stuart Brown writes from a unique design perspective; he makes tools for extremely specialized surgeons. In this chapter, he considers the dynamics of working for such 'high value, time-poor' and often headstrong clients and discusses the necessity of considering the whole context of a very bespoke device—pointing out, for example, that the cleaner of the tool may be as important to consider as the surgeon. The conundrum he discusses is that 'the highly performing product [the pioneering surgeon seeks] requires significant input from them to ensure that it matches their needs and expectations, but their busy lives do not afford them the luxury of contributing significantly to the design process'. Various surgical instrument examples are offered before Brown directs the discussion towards the generic value of the 'thought experiment'.

In the chapter 'Computer-embedded Design: PAIPR Prototyping', product designer Steve Gill draws on his work on physicality and the experience of touch, discussing methods by which prototyping can be used to anticipate and structure tactile experiences in subsequent objects. Gill discusses some of the issues industrial designers currently face when they wish to prototype information appliances. He posits a need for change within the design process and the development of new tools to support effective design for computer-embedded products. Through an essentially technical design discussion, Gill shares five lessons learned by PAIPR on the practical issues of speed and fit, capability, physicality and scale, screens and education for researchers when investigating future prototyping methodologies. In conclusion, he questions the current global preference to employ multidisciplinary teams of people to design computer-embedded products.

The penultimate chapter by Rosan Chow, a design theorist, challenges the contemporaneous approach to designing, which predominantly begins by understanding user needs and user contexts. She notes that design conventions (such as beginning designing by understanding user needs) are useful, but they are not always appropriate, especially when working with indeterminate problems. Chow distils a necessary tension in the act of designing: the physical, conceptual and perceptual struggle between language and metalanguage. She presents Charles Sanders Peirce's system of signs (where signs are forms of abductive, inductive and deductive reasoning) as valuable to the design and development of new products and categories of product. In her chapter 'The RIP+MIX Method and Reflection on its Prototypes', Chow's new products of 'Case Transfer' and 'Rip and Mix' are central to the discussion and used to expose her theory in practice. Chow argues for the application of semiotic theory to be applied to the problem of product development, where product includes design research method(s).

In the closing remark, Louise Valentine argues that in this new phase of social and cultural change, it is important to understand the concepts that traverse the world of making and to understand the significance of intellectual space(s) that exist between discipline boundaries. Valentine argues that the space(s) in-between people and their disciplines is a chance to critically explore new ways of building effective systems for participatory cross-cultural working. Through the 'Prototype', her intention is to offer a means with which to rethink our values, suggesting greater emphasis should be placed on testing alternative methodologies and methods for craft innovation, including group work outside of the traditional craft knowledge domain frameworks. In doing so, she attends to the growing need for designers and craftspeople to work together and share insights between specialisms as well as within them. The discussion closes by presenting key insights gained from working within diverse fields in relation to the prototype as a language and concept.

CONCLUSION

Prototype is concerned with how design and craft might cooperate, communicate and collaborate in this next phase of globalization. There are many exemplary writings exposing the nature of design and the nature of craft. Indeed, the first decade of the twenty-first century witnessed an explosion in both volume and quality of literature, through, for example, the works of Glenn Adamson, Richard Buchanan, Rachel Cooper, Ken Friedman, Tony Fry, Ulla Johansson, Lucy Kimbell, Klaus Krippendorf, Ezio Manzini, Bill Moggridge, Howard Risatti and Richard Sennett.

The premise behind this collection is to share and build upon contemporary commentary, recognizing the value in crossing boundaries to refresh our thinking, find hidden assumptions and seek solutions to problems. It is concerned with offering an alternative way to question and communicate craft and design; it can be viewed as a prototype itself.

NOTE

1. *Craft as a Form of Mindful Inquiry* was the postdoctoral study within the major project, *Past, Present and Future Craft Practice*. Coauthored with Professor Georgina Follett in 2004, the £442K funding was awarded through the responsive-type support where individuals make a direct application to a research council, specifically the Arts and Humanities Research Council in this instance. Professor Georgina Follett is a deputy principal of the University of Dundee, Scotland and was principal investigator of the *Past, Present and Future Craft Practice*. Georgina is a contemporary craft practitioner of forty years, specializing in plique-à-jour enamelling. Born in London, she is a graduate of the Royal College of Art. Her practitioner portfolio specializes in plique-à-jour enamelled jewellery in precious metals: a system of using enamel within jewellery to give a stained glass effect. She is the only practitioner of this way of working in the UK and one of a handful in Europe. Her work is held in many private collections as well as permanent ones, such as the Roy Strong collections in the Victoria and Albert Museum, and the National Museums of Scotland. She is an

indexed member of the Crafts Council and a Fellow of the Royal Society of Arts and Manufacturers, The Chartered Society of Designers and a Founding Fellow of the Institute of Contemporary Scotland. In 2007 Georgina Follett was awarded an OBE in the Queen's Birthday Honours.

FURTHER READING

Alvesson, M., and Sköldberg, K. (2009), *Reflexive Methodology: New Vistas for Qualitative Research*, 2nd edn, Los Angeles: Sage.

Bentz, V. M., and Shapiro, B. (1998), *Mindful Inquiry in Social Research*, Newbury Park: Sage.

Borja de Mozota, B. (2006), 'The Four Powers of Design: A Value Model in Design Management', *Design Management Review*, 17/2: 44–53.

Brown, H. (2008), *Knowledge and Innovation: A Comparative Study of the USA, the UK and Japan*, London: Routledge.

Brown, T. (2009), *Change by Design: How Design Thinking Transforms Organizations and Inspires Innovation*, New York: HarperCollins.

Buchanan, R., Doordan, D., and Margolin, V. (eds) (2010), *The Designed World: Images, Objects, Environments*, Oxford: Berg.

Crotty, M. (1998), *The Foundations of Social Research: Meaning and Perspective in the Research Process*, Los Angeles: Sage.

Dunne, A. (2005), *Hertzian Tales: Electronic Products, Aesthetic Experience, and Critical Design*, Cambridge, MA: MIT Press.

Evans, M. (2011), 'Empathising with the Future: Creating Next-Next Generation Products and Services', *The Design Journal, Special Issue: Design + Empathy*, 14/2: 231–52.

Fry, T. (2009), *Design Futuring: Sustainability, Ethics and New Practice*, Oxford: Berg.

Inns, T. (ed.) (2010), *Designing for the 21st Century: Interdisciplinary Methods and Findings*, London: Gower.

Inns, T., Baxter, S., and Murphy, E. (2006), 'Transfer or Emergence: Strategies for Building Design Knowledge through Knowledge Transfer Partnerships', *The Design Journal*, 9/3: 34–44.

Jahnke, M. (2012), 'Revisiting Design as a Hermeneutic Practice: An Investigation of Paul Ricoeur's Critical Hermeneutics', *Design Issues*, 28/2: 30–40.

Kimbell, L. (2011), 'Rethinking Design Thinking: Part 1', *Design and Culture*, 3/3: 285–306.

Koskinen, I., Zimmerman, J., Binder, T., Redström, J., and Wensveen, S. (2011), *Design Research Through Practice: From the Lab, Field, and Showroom*, New York: Morgan Kaufman.

Krippendorf, K. (2006), *The Semantic Turn: A New Foundation for Design*, Boca Raton, FL: Taylor & Francis.

Peat, F. D. (2008), *Gentle Action: Bringing Creative Change to a Turbulent World*, Pari, Italy: Pari.

Redström, J. (2006), 'Towards User Design? On the Shift from Object to User as the Subject of Design', *Design Studies*, 27/2: 123–39.

Schrage, M. (2000), *Serious Play: How the World's Best Companies Simulate to Innovate*, Boston, MA: Harvard Business Press.

Stickdorn, M., and Schneider, J. (2011), *This is Service Design*, Hoboken, NJ: John Wiley & Sons.

Ulrich, K. T., and Eppinger, S. D. (2003), *Product Design and Development*, 3rd edn, New York: McGraw Hill.

Valentine, L. (2004), 'The Activity of Rhetoric within the Process of a Designer's Thinking', PhD thesis, University of Dundee, Scotland.

Valentine, L. (2010), 'Past and Present Craft Practice: A Frame of Reference for Mindful Inquiry Research and Future Craft', in L. Valentine and G. Follett (eds), *Past, Present and Future Craft Practice*, Edinburgh: National Museums Scotland Ltd.

Valentine, L. (2011), 'Craft as a Form of Mindful Inquiry', *The Design Journal*, 14/3: 283–306.

1 CRAFTING INTERACTIONS: THE PURPOSE AND PRACTICE OF SERIOUS PLAY

MICHAEL SCHRAGE

The year 2010 marked the seventy-fifth anniversary of the Daventry Experiment—an experiment linked directly to Dundee, Scotland in the person of Sir Robert Watson-Watt and arguably the most important 'rapid prototyping' improvisation in British history.

Whipped up with oscilloscopes, borrowed BBC aerials and a Handley Page Heyford bomber, the experiment was an 'actions speak louder than calculations' demonstration. On 26 February 1935 the scepticism of Hugh Dowding of Fighter Command about his boffins' pencil and paper analyses disappeared. The Daventry Experiment revealed that radio waves could informationally empower an air defence system. Radio Direction Finding—Radar—worked.

This crude prototype became a critical springboard for launching systemic technological innovation. Innovative interaction around innovative prototypes helped ensure victory in the Battle of Britain and beyond. The craft of rapid prototyping drove British innovation throughout the war (Bragg 2002; Watson-Watt 1957).

The vignette makes an oft-underappreciated point about the real-world context of prototype design. Prototypes are as much cultural artefacts as technical objects. They reflect individual ingenuity as much as they embody institutional imperatives. Successful prototypes invite and encourage serious play. The prototype becomes as much a medium of interpersonal interaction as a tool for discovery, insight and test.

The prototyping ethos that turned numerical squiggles on paper into the Chain Home radar networks had its sociointellectual roots in one of Watson-Watt's ancestors—James Watt. Watt's original interest in steam engine design came directly from his efforts to fix a model of a Newcomen engine for the University of Glasgow. Playing with the model steam engine led to insights suggesting a separate condenser. Watt made practical his epiphany by using a brass surgeon's syringe to quickly prototype his model piston (Hills 1993; Marsden 2002).

Iterative prototyping, modelling and scientific analysis converged into the creation of steam engines that effectively powered the Industrial Revolution. Watt and Matthew Boulton mastered both the business and process of profitable prototyping. Along with other innovators, such as John Wilkinson, they collaboratively prototyped their way into a new era of global productivity.

The times, technologies and temperaments may have been fundamentally different, but a shared willingness and ability to seriously play with prototypes made transformative innovations, such as steam engines and radar, possible. The craft of prototyping transcends time and technology.

These historical and British examples define the narrative spine of this prototyping chapter. Prototypes are wonderful windows and lenses with which to view the people and processes of innovation. This chapter's purpose is to identify and outline fundamental principles of the craft and culture of prototyping. The argument is that the craft of prototyping is best understood in the context of crafting hypotheses, crafting marketplaces and crafting 'playgrounds'. Prototypes are hypotheses, prototypes are marketplaces and prototypes are playgrounds.

My own initial curiosity around prototyping stemmed from my time at Massachusetts Institute of Technology's (MIT) Media Lab. The Lab's motto twisted the scholarly cliché of 'Publish or Perish' into 'Demo or Die'. Creating a provocative demo was more important than writing a publishable paper. Professors and graduate students alike were thus constantly demoing their prototypes to colleagues, peer reviewers, sponsors and the public.

I quickly observed clear cultural and behavioural distinctions in demoing: the majority of demos were classic show and tell exhibitions; they illustrated the conceptual brilliance and cleverness of the prototyper. For want of a better phrase, these demos were sales pitches.

The more intriguing demos, however, were the show and asks. Soliciting comment and eliciting feedback mattered more than winning 'oohs and aahs' of admiration. I was struck by how conversations and interactions around prototypes seemed richer, more dynamic and—frankly—more creative than sales pitches. Interactions around artefacts looked, felt and sounded different from other interactions. That fascinated me. That fascination led to extensive research and advisory work around the notion of prototypes as shared spaces for iterative interaction and innovation.

The classic craft view of prototypes sees them as artefacts. These artefacts capture the design intent of their creators. But this conventionally accurate view does not go far enough. Prototypes are not just about crafting artefacts; they inherently craft interactions between people. Prototypes are as much media for human interaction as technical effect.

My observation is that the real value of a prototype comes less from its instantiation and reification than the interpersonal interactions it inspires. Prototypes are media—places and platforms for collaborative creativity. They enable different ecologies and economies of innovation insight. They are means to interpersonal—not just technical—ends.

The best prototypes—the best models of reality—have charisma. In football, basketball, ice-hockey or any team sport, there are always players whose talents tower above the rest. But a rare handful of superstars—Pelé, 'Magic' Johnson, Wayne Gretzky—are not only individually great but somehow make everyone around them play better and accomplish more. They have a charisma that compels overachievement by others. It is a fantastic quality.

The best prototypes are comparably motivational and inspirational. Call them 'charismodels'—prototypes exuding a charisma that inspires people interacting with them to think better, create better and innovate better.

Charismodels are artefacts that get people to ask questions or explore opportunities that ordinarily would not come to mind. As with great works of art, charismodels let people see new possibilities with new eyes. They forge communities of interest and practice. This was as true for Watt's steam engine in the eyes of Matthew Boulton as it was for Watson-Watt's radar in the mind of Hugh Dowding and Henry Tizard.

Crafting charismatic prototypes is not the purpose or the goal, however. The prototype is a means, medium and mechanism towards an innovative end. Great prototypes typically lead to great outcomes.

Just as charismatic athletes lift the level of play, charismatic prototypes elevate the quality of creativity. Craft in this context goes beyond refinement of detail towards enhancement of concept. Great prototypes facilitate both.

What elements of craft promote conceptual enhancement and technical refinement? Three organising design principles merit special focus: (*a*) a prototype is a hypothesis, (*b*) a prototype is a marketplace and (*c*) a prototype is a playground.

Each principle deserves detailed examination. Prototyping craft is the story of the sensibility, technique and care brought to managing how these principles intersect. Prototypes may reflect any one or all of these three themes. But their dynamic interaction offers the greatest opportunities for excitement, ingenuity, creativity and impact. Their dynamic interaction shapes craft.

A PROTOTYPE IS A HYPOTHESIS

Conventional wisdom sees prototypes as models—selective slivers of possible reality. American historian of technology Thomas Hughes once described prototypes as slices of 'congealed culture'. All true.

Every prototype is also a hypothesis. That is a prototype is a proposition explicitly designed to explain—or make an educated guess about—an observable phenomenon.

The dictionary definition of 'hypothesis'[1] suggests as much:

1. A proposition, or set of propositions, set forth as an explanation for the occurrence of some specified group of phenomena, either asserted merely as a provisional conjecture to guide investigation (working hypothesis) or accepted as highly probable in the light of established facts.
2. A proposition assumed as a premise in an argument.
3. The antecedent of a conditional proposition.
4. A mere assumption or guess.

Calling a prototype a hypothesis means that prototypes are educated guesses about the future—the future of how the prototype might perform, the future of how potential users might react to it, the future of how it might be produced or manufactured, the future of how people might sell or market it, the future of how researchers might further explore and test its technical features and functionalities, the future of how designers might further shape or refine its look, and so forth. The prototype describes a potential future worth testing.

A prototype's design hypothesis is an assertion of how a design choice creates value, that is 'What option do you like more?' and/or 'How do we design this better?' The prototype embodies the design hypotheses to be tested.

The Apple™ iPad prototype was an excruciatingly well-crafted hypothesis about the future of digital media consumption. An Android phone prototype is a superbly educated guess about mobile communications. No doubt, prototypes of a future Toyota Prius will set forth important propositions about the future of four-wheeled carbon neutral transport.

In other words, prototypes inherently embody the propositions, antecedents, assumptions and guesses that define a hypothesis. Crafting a prototype—digital, physical or virtual—means crafting a hypothesis. If there is no hypothesis, then there is no prototype. The more refined the hypothesis, the more refined the prototype. The more speculative the hypothesis, the more speculative the prototype.

But a hypothesis for whom? Does the hypothesis/prototype have the user in mind first? The manufacturing team? The interface designer? The accountants? The sales people? Or all of them?

Who gets to formulate the hypothesis? Who owns it? How will it be tested? These simple and straightforward questions quickly bring to the surface the cultural and organizational tensions confronting all design communities. Are the hypotheses rooted in market, technical or aesthetic concerns? Are the hypotheses managed as an integrated portfolio of educated guesses? Or is each hypothesis the equivalent of a requirement or spec demanding confirmation and compliance?

As with any physics, chemistry or biology experiment, the prototype is meant to do more than articulate and test a hypothesis. It is also intended to persuade. A successful prototype—like a successful experimental hypothesis—effectively persuades people of its value and rightness. A prototype that does not persuade—like an experiment that does not support its hypothesis—is seen as a failure. Successful prototypes win in the marketplace of ideas.

A PROTOTYPE IS A MARKETPLACE

Many design and engineering schools define prototypes as the deliberate products of structured design processes. Just as audits are the result of auditing processes or new hires are outcomes of personnel processes, prototypes emerge from replicable and repeatable innovation processes. For most organizations, this conventional view captures the reality appropriately.

My empirical research proffers an alternate view. This interpretation sees prototypes emerging from less structured and more informal processes—processes that mimic market mechanisms. Prototypes are not just organizational artefacts and media for interaction; they are actually marketplaces—a space, place and medium where value is negotiated and exchanged.

In this context, prototypes become vehicles and venues where designers, engineers, manufacturers, programmers, marketers, finance people, and so on gather to trade, exchange and add value to the proposed product or service. The prototype is like a souk or stock exchange where people come to negotiate value. This feature is traded off against that function; by removing this option, we will make the prototype 30 per cent easier to use, and so on. The prototyping 'tradespace' mirrors the dealings and design conflicts that determine its ultimate form. Sometimes better negotiations lead to better features, functionality and aesthetics; other times, it is vice versa.

The prototype becomes the symbol and substance of market processes regulated by the organizational, cultural and economic norms of the enterprise. Some of these are informal—or even slightly illicit—grey markets. Other market mechanisms—transfer pricing, for example—could not be more legalistic.

Instead of prototypes being extruded like plastic by a prototyping process, they *are* the innovation process. The prototype drives the process; it is not just a process result. Yes, design sequences and checklists demanding rigorous compliance exist. But market metaphors ask designers and innovators to see prototypes as innovation currencies facilitating trade between organizational marketplaces and marketplaces beyond the enterprise.

Toyota has exceptionally disciplined processes for the design of its cars. Yet its automotive prototypes are profoundly influenced and reshaped by how they engage with the larger Toyota enterprise economy and their exposure to external market forces. Changes in the internal Toyota economy and the external global economy alter design trade-offs made in Toyota's prototypes. Similarly, Web 2.0 companies, such as Google and Amazon, see their software prototypes iteratively evolve as a function of use. As publisher and pundit Tim O'Reilly (2004) puts it, Web 2.0 affects an 'architecture of participation' that delivers software as a service 'that gets better the more people use it'.

In other words, Web 2.0 is a marketplace structured to ensure that greater participation adds greater value to the products and services provided. The innovation has a perpetual beta/never-finished quality. Web 2.0 offerings are deliberately crafted as dynamic marketplaces in their own right. The more people interact with them, the more valuable they become for everyone. Google's search algorithms and Amazon's recommendation engines are perpetual prototypes and dynamic marketplaces. They invite new value to be created, negotiated and shared.

In my advisory work, I frequently ask organization leaders: what kind of marketplaces are your prototypes? Are your prototyping marketplaces governed more by the values of an Adam Smith or a Karl Marx? Are they laissez-faire markets reflecting free and fair exchange?

Do top-down edicts consistently overrule bottom-up opportunity? Are prototypes strictly regulated markets with rigid rules and restrictions set down by Finance and Headquarters? Or do business units have discretion over how they use their prototypes to collaborate with customers, clients and each other? Does centralized planning or distributed empowerment rule prototype development?

Are your prototypes like pre-Glasnost Gosplans that define any improvisation or variation as deviance? Are prototypes the products of design principles that reflect and respect the cultural values of the enterprise? Or do they reflect conformance to compliance checklists for new product development in formal innovation processes?

Not a single one of these questions is rhetorical or hypothetical. On the contrary, the prototype as marketplace metaphor forces organizations to revisit their most fundamental assumptions around how they want to innovate.

The Daventry Experiment begat a host of insights generating insight far beyond the physics and electronics of radio waves; it forced organizational innovations and experiments that made Fighter Command possible. This was a prototyping marketplace that struck a marvellously productive tension between bottom-up opportunism and top-down strategic intent.

Watson's separate condenser—and the reinvention of steam's efficiencies as a prime mover—led to new markets and new business models, not just new technologies: prototypes created new relationships between people as well as new applications of technology. Boulton and Watt's collaborative genius made their prototypes and prototyping a market mechanism for customized collaboration with their customers. This was integral to their success.

A PROTOTYPE IS A PLAYGROUND

In his 1908 essay 'Creative Writing and Day Dreaming', Freud observed that 'The opposite of play is not what is serious but what is real' (143). That is, 'play' represents a surreal, unreal or 'not quite' reality. There is a freedom in the notion that non reality does not just permit but actually encourages creativity and dreaming. The writer, the artist, the talented craftsperson, ultimately makes the product of play real, but that emergent aesthetic reality could never have been possible without playing.

In James March's 1979 article 'The Technology of Foolishness', the Stanford University management guru defined play as 'a deliberate, temporary relaxation of rules in order to explore the possibilities of alternate rules'. In other words, pace Freud, play offers opportunities to safely explore and engage alternatives. Play is a process that can give rise to new realities.

That makes prototypes playgrounds. Prototypes are not yet real. Prototypes are places where—by design—the rules are relaxed to explore alternatives. At the core of every child's playground is a design ethos encouraging energy, exuberance and engagement. Prototypes are playgrounds for innovators with similar sensibilities and desires. Playgrounds and prototypes are both media where cooperation, collaboration and imagination animate interpersonal interaction. The purpose of the prototype as playground is the freedom to go beyond known norms and standards to innovate and create.

This freedom possesses an important design attribute. The improvisations and outcomes of play are inherently unpredictable. If the improvisations and outcomes are known in advance, it is not really play. Uncertainty is essential to successful play. The unexpected and unanticipated are intrinsic to the experience. Surprise can be an enemy as well as a friend, but you cannot know the outcome unless and until you play. This holds equally true when playing with prototypes. There is no play in building a prototype to specification. There is no uncertainty in conforming to requirements; that is the antithesis of play. Playing with prototypes means bidding for serendipity and discovery. Prototypes as playgrounds is a bet that loosening reality's rules will lead to a better-designed reality.

My own work defines play as 'an active engagement in riskless competition between speculative alternatives' (Schrage 2000, 2001).[2] This definition explicitly respects a dominant concern and constraint confronting individuals and organizations striving to innovate; that is risk. Successfully—and safely—managing risk is a major imperative for many design organizations. Consequently, prototypes are often seen as media and mechanisms for managing design and innovation risk.

That presents a tension. Implicit in both Freud and March is a sentiment that play should be safe. That is, playing with a concept or an idea is not inherently dangerous or destructive. On the contrary, play is typically celebrated as a low-risk/high-impact way to bring creative value and imagination to reality. If play was truly dangerous, it would not be play; it would be a threat—a potentially harmful risk.

This conjures up the play paradox—an insight that explains why the prototype as playground metaphor is destined to assume greater prominence. Play is typically seen as fun, whimsical, unreal and fundamentally unserious. Many organizations and individuals honestly believe that serious and sophisticated analyses offer better ways to manage innovation risk than play. Serious risk is serious business. Play detracts and distracts.

The opposite is true: organizations are not being serious about either innovation or risk unless they play. That is, unless innovators play—in the Freudian and Marchian sense of loosening the strictures of known realities—they cheat themselves out of the serendipitous insight, and they insulate themselves from the unpleasant surprise.

Play should present a safe way to raise unexpected and/or unanticipated risks. Prototypes should represent safe media to experience flaws and failures found through play. Innovation and risk are opposite sides of the same coin. Prototypes are playgrounds where innovators can discover—to their pleasure and horror—what relaxation of rules lead to which possible realities.

This raises questions about the crafting of playgrounds that complement the questions discussed about the crafting of marketplaces. What kind of prototyping playgrounds do we wish to create? How fun and inviting do we want them to be? Are we comfortable with the possibility that people might really hurt themselves playing with them? Are these playgrounds that encourage participants to play with each other? Or should they each keep to their section? How much of a learning or educational experience should the playground provide? Is there enough adult supervision? Or too much?

What should be strikingly clear is that ecologies of prototype as playground powerfully influence economies of prototype as marketplace. The hypotheses that prototypes embody may enjoy—or endure—different experiences in the marketplace as opposed to the playground—and vice versa. The prototype steam engine experiences life differently as an artefact in a playground than as a hypothesis in a marketplace. The radar hypothesis in a prototyping playground yields opportunities differently than its artefact in the Second World War procurement marketplace.

In a digitized era where virtual prototypes and software artefacts outnumber their physical counterparts, the dynamic interactions between hypothesis, marketplace and playground become even more acute. Architectural issues of interoperability and integration assume greater design prominence. The craft of prototyping respects a desire to ensure that prototypes can move seamlessly within and between their roles as hypotheses, marketplaces and playgrounds.

More importantly, perhaps, the craft of prototyping increasingly means focusing one's design attentions—and intentions—upon the hypotheses, marketplaces and playgrounds themselves. That is, how do changes in marketplace regulations or playground rules influence interactions between people and their iteratively evolving prototypes?

There is a temptingly comfortable perception that our processes drive our prototypes. When one really examines actual behaviours, the opposite seems closer to the mark: our prototypes drive our processes. Changes in the prototype directly shape our hypotheses, our market perceptions and how—and with whom—we wish to play.

Indeed, one of the great business clichés is that innovative teams generate innovative prototypes. Again, the opposite seems more respectful of the truth: innovative prototypes generate innovative teams. Prototypes frequently serve as lures and bait for creative contribution by others. The artefact becomes, in essence, an innovation invitation for hypothesis, play and value exchange.

Craft is often defined as skilful making. The thrust of this paper and the sweep of innovation history suggest that the craft of prototyping is as much about the skilful making of hypotheses, markets and playful interaction as the painstaking construction of artefacts.

The future craft of prototyping design will be found in the future of hypothesis design, the future of marketplace design and the future of play. That is an excellent future to have.

NOTES

1. See dictionary.com.
2. Quote from a lecture by the author Schrage, M., 'Rethinking "Serious Play"', lecture given at The Power of Play conference, Stanford University, CA, 9 October 2004. Available at: http://news.stanford.edu/news/2004/october20/play-1020.html, accessed 9 September 2013.

FURTHER READING

Bragg, M.W. (2002), *RDF 1—The Location of Aircraft by Radio Methods 1935–1945*, Paisley, Scotland: Hawkhead.

Freud, S. ([1908] 1974), 'Creative Writers and Day-Dreaming', in *The Standard Edition of the Complete Psychological Works of Sigmund Freud, Volume IX (1906–1908): Jensen's 'Gradiva' and Other Works*, London: Hogarth, 141–54.

Hills, R.L. (1993), *Power from Steam: A History of the Stationary Steam Engine*, Cambridge, UK: Cambridge University Press.

March, James G. (1979), 'The Technology of Foolishness', in J.G. March and J. Olsen (eds), *Ambiguity and Choice in Organizations*, 2nd edn, Bergen: Universitetsforlaget, Chapter 5.

Marsden, B. (2002), *Watt's Perfect Engine: Steam and the Age of Invention (Revolutions in Science)*, New York: Columbia University Press.

O'Reilly, T. (2004), 'The Architecture of Participation', O'Reilly, http://oreilly.com/pub/a/oreilly/tim/articles/architecture_of_participation.html, accessed 8 December 2010.

Schrage, M. (2000), *Serious Play: How the World's Best Companies Simulate to Innovate*, Boston, MA: Harvard Business School Press.

Schrage, M. (2001), 'Here Comes Hyperinnovation', *strategy+business*, 22, http://www.strategy-business.com/article/10900?gko=ttp:/, accessed 8 December 2010.

Watson-Watt, R.A. (1957), *Three Steps to Victory: A Personal Account by Radar's Greatest Pioneer*, London: Odhams Press.

2 FROM MARI TO MEMPHIS: THE ROLE OF PROTOTYPES IN ITALIAN RADICAL AND POSTMODERN DESIGN

CATHARINE ROSSI

On its debut at the 1981 Milan furniture fair, the brash, bright furniture of the first Memphis collection provoked extreme reactions. For Karl Lagerfeld, it was 'love at first sight' (Anon. 1991: 5); so enamoured was the German fashion designer that he furnished his entire Monte Carlo apartment with the imaginings of the international design collective. A few years later he sold it all off; a move not surprising for a design collective that aspired to the life cycle of fashion, to be the New International Style.

Memphis had been dreamt up less than a year earlier during a series of evenings at the Milanese home of the architect Ettore Sottsass in December 1980. Its name came up during one of these mythical get-togethers; playing on repeat in the background was Bob Dylan's 1966 record *Stuck Inside of Mobile with the Memphis Blues Again*. Around thirty international designers and architects would sign up to the Memphis group, including Michael Graves, Michele De Lucchi, Hans Hollein and Martine Bedin. Together, they contributed fifty-five examples of furniture, clocks, glass and ceramics that were then unveiled at Milan's Arc '74 showroom.

This was furniture that deliberately broke the rules. It trod over the canons of good taste and the modernist myth of good design and distanced itself from a postmodernism of neoclassicism and historical pastiche. Instead, Memphis offered furniture covered in plastic laminates and fabrics whose patterns, such as Sottsass's 'Casablanca' sideboard (Figure 2.1), combined everything from Primitivism to Pop, real marble and fake finishes and clashed acid yellows and violent pinks—a pluralism that confirmed their postmodern credentials. These were designs to be photographed, to be looked at, and they were deliberately endowed with an attention-grabbing quality confirmed by the media frenzy that quickly erupted. With hundreds of articles, exhibitions, copies, famous owners and film appearances, the Memphis designs were soon celebrities in their own right.

Figure 2.1　Ettore Sottsass, 'Casablanca' sideboard, Memphis, 1981. © Victoria and Albert Museum, London.

But despite their familiarity, one aspect of the Memphis furniture has been overlooked—their condition as one-off, handcrafted prototypes, one-of-a-kind provisional ideas palmed off as finished products. For this first collection—there would be five until the group was officially disbanded in 1987—nothing came before or after. There were no construction drawings, no models, no developments—a transition from sketch to smash hit in less than a year.

Of course, Memphis was not the first design phenomenon to rely on the prototype. In many ways, it had been the default status of design in postwar Italy, the objects photographed for the articles and adverts in design magazines, such as *Domus* and *Casabella*, and shown in international showcases, such as the annual furniture fair and the *Triennale di Milano*, the exhibition of design and architecture held every three years in the city until 1996. Designed for publicity as much as for production, the prototype contributed to the huge international success of Italy's postwar generations of architects and designers.

The prototype also spoke of the intimate and underrecognized relationship between design and craft in postwar Italy. In 1981, the same year of Memphis's debut, the Italian architect Enzo Mari curated an exhibition that asked *Where is the Craftsman?* (Mari 1981). In the postindustrial context of the early 1980s the answer was surprisingly positive: Italy's furniture and apparel industries were dominated by a network of small-scale artisanal enterprises. These workshops were equally important when it came to factory production; much of Mari's exhibition was devoted to the role of those artisans responsible for dies, moulds, patterns, models and prototypes that made industrial manufacture possible.

Yet the prototype, of vital importance to Italy's postwar design story, has been overlooked. Arguably, this is not surprising. On the one hand, the success of Italian design becomes a lot more uncertain when it becomes clear that many of its iconic objects never even went into production. On the other, in the context of the Italian furniture industry, the prototype was an object handmade by craft practitioners. As such, the lack of recognition for its role becomes shorthand for the marginalization of craft as a whole in Italian design historiography.

This paper concentrates on one aspect of this story. In the growing crisis that defined Italian design from the late 1960s to early 1980s, the prototype played a central role as a polemical and increasingly publicity-driven type of object, one at the centre of design and craft's relationship. This shifting role of the prototype in Italian radical and postmodern design can only be understood in light of the roles the prototype performed in the earlier postwar period. Once these are established, the reason why the Memphis objects were prototypes—and why this mattered—should become clear.

ADVANCED TECHNOLOGY AND ARTISANAL TECHNIQUES: PROTOTYPES IN ITALIAN DESIGN, 1945 TO 1960

The seeds for the different roles that the prototype took on in Italian radical and postmodern design were sown some thirty years earlier. Design was part of the larger project of postwar reconstruction. Without any discrete design pedagogy or profession until the 1960s, it was Italy's architects who were designing furniture to rebuild the nation and set the template for Italy's emergence on the international marketplace. As such, the production of prototypes was geared towards developing another object type: the archetype.

The interplay between archetype and prototype was most explicit in the 'Superleggera' (Figure 2.2). Designed by the Milanese architect Gio Ponti, this chair is one of the so-called icons of Italian design, produced by Cassina from 1957 and still in production today. This chair was the result of a quest for ever-increasing lightness that inspired much of Ponti's work, from the slender

Figure 2.2   Gio Ponti's *Superleggera* chair mid-air above the Cassina factory, in a demonstration of its strength and lightness. © Archivio Storico Cassina.

Pirelli skyscraper in Milan (1956–60) to the Taranto Cathedral in the South of Italy (1970).

It took nearly ten years of sketches, design drawings and prototypes to get to be *superleggera*—beyond lightness. The first version of the chair, in painted ash with brass-tipped legs from 1949, was made by Giordano Chiesa, a furniture maker who Ponti repeatedly turned to for prototypes and one-off commissions. By 1951 it had become the 'Leggera' (light), put into production following the extensive technical innovation needed to achieve the desire for conjoined actual and formal lightness.

This combination of manufacturers willing to invest in product development and skilled artisans available to translate designs into objects would become a hallmark of Italian manufacturing. The 1950s may have been marked by a wave of industrialization, the latest in what had been a staggered and fragmented process, but it remained a localized phenomenon, dominated by the industrial triangle of Genoa, Milan and Turin in which craft skills and processes remained vital. Certainly the furniture industry, centred in the Milanese hinterland of Brianza, remained predominantly artisanal in character.

This widespread availability of craft production in Italy often translated into artisans' skills and ongoing traditions being taken for granted. In 1952, when the chair was still just the 'Leggera', Ponti was already speaking of its archetypal status. In an article in *Domus*, the magazine he edited from its foundation in 1928 until his death in 1979, Ponti (1952: 1) wrote an article called 'Without Adjectives' in which he differentiates between his chair and what he calls 'haughty chairs with adjectives'—although a plethora are used in the article. He describes it as a 'chair-chair', 'the true "chair of always", the chair that was already there, the pre-existing chair'. Ponti rejects antecedents, and adjectives are rejected in order to make the 'Leggera' into an archetype; Ponti invites readers to follow him, to produce 'beds-beds, wardrobes-wardrobes', and so on.

However, the 'Leggera' was not an archetype. On the one hand, it was a prototype—the 'Superleggera' was yet to come. Moreover, despite Ponti's claims, there was a preexisting chair—the 'Chiavari' chair, a smart straw-seated ladder-back chair from the Ligurian coast in production since the 1800s. This chair enjoyed renewed popularity in the early 1950s and was featured in exhibitions of Italian design in which it was described as the *leggerissima* (lightest) chair. Ponti even relied on the continuing production of these chairs for the manufacturing of the 'Superleggera'. Mass produced in the Cassina factory—itself a site of craftsmanship—the chair seat was handwoven by female pieceworkers in the Chiavari hinterland. This labour-intensive production process contributed to the chair's status as an unwittingly expensive, luxury object available only to the few rather than the desired masses.

The 1950s was defined by this faith in industrial production that fell down when confronted with Italy's inability to produce or consume on a modern, mass scale. It was also seen in furniture such as the 'San Luca' armchair from 1959, designed by Achille and Pier Giacomo Castiglioni and produced by Gavina. In the 'San Luca', traditional upholstery was rejected in favour of innovative rubber padding. Paradoxically, this use of advanced materials necessitated manual production, as the chair was composed of a series of separate padded components, which had to be constructed and finished individually before being screwed together. Mari included the 'San Luca' in his 1981 exhibition as an example of a quasi prototype, 'designed to be mass-produced but in fact manufactured one or two at a time, and only to order' (Mari 1981: 44).

The 'San Luca' was designed at the peak of Italy's mythical economic miracle, or boom, the years between 1958 and 1962 in which the nation explosively emerged as a productive and consumer power. Italian design served up an image of elegance to cement its international prestige and meet the desires of the nation's newfound image of consumerist prosperity. In this luxury turn, materials such as leather and marble became what the design historian Penny Sparke has called the '*sine qua non*' of Italian design (Sparke 1990: 178). So pervasive was the logic of luxury that architects, such as Vico Magistretti, even turned their attention to that most inauspicious of materials—plastics—to producing synthetic furnishings every bit a part of *la dolce vita* as the shoes of Salvatore Ferragamo or the cinema of Federico Fellini.

This modern, industrial material still demanded artisanal knowledge and a close dialogue between architect and artisan. So complex was the *s* shaped section of the 'Selene' that Magistretti (Pasca 1991: 49) said 'it couldn't be drawn', and so instead he turned to a 'sublime' model maker to visualize and develop his design. As the craft practitioner and theorist David Pye (1968: 75) described, craft skills do not disappear in industrial production but instead relocate to the 'preparatory' phases of which prototypes, moulds and tooling are all part.

POLEMICAL PROTOTYPES: ITALIAN RADICAL DESIGN

The miracle did not last long. By the mid-1960s inflation, unemployment, high levels of internal migration and a lack of investment in public infrastructure were joined by increasing international disaffection with the modern consumer society. In this first wave of what would be known as radical, or anti- or counter-design, Italy's avant-garde architects responded with objects that ironically engaged with the mass consumerist language of kitsch and Pop and anticipated the populist references of the postmodern style. In recognition of this, Sottsass (Nelson 1983) would later describe the 'very strange' brightly coloured striped laminate 'Superboxes' (Figure 2.3) from 1966 as representing the origins of Memphis.

The inclusion of the 'Superboxes' in *Domus* spread awareness of the increasingly contestatory stance of Italy's avant-garde. Framed by a series of furnishings, including rugs and hi-fis, the Superboxes proposed a new aesthetic for the domestic interior. However, despite their appearance, these were not 1:1 scale prototypes but miniature models. The furnishings were in fact miniature props—doll-house pieces bought from a Milanese toy store that gave the illusion of full-sized rooms.

By the early 1970s full scale-versions were produced for exhibition purposes. Several years later the 'Superboxes' were put into production, a shift that transformed these models retrospectively into prototypes. This time lag between appearance and production is telling. Ultimately, it speaks of a shift in emphasis amongst Italy's radical architects. Design was no longer about making prototypes, let alone archetypes. Instead, it was about an open-ended exploration with more conceptual and behavioural aims.

Figure 2.3   Ettore Sottsass, *Superbox*, designed in 1966. © Maria Assunta Radice, Sottsass Archive.

The same was true of the Archizoom Associati, the radical group established in 1966 by the young Florentine architects Andrea Branzi, Gilberto Corretti, Paolo Deganello and Massimo Morozzi. Like the 'Superboxes', their 'Dream Beds' (1967) appeared in *Domus*, and these too were miniature models in carefully choreographed fictional set-ups. For a generation of architects largely out of work and increasingly reluctant to engage with the mechanisms of mass production and consumption, the small-scale model made sense. It was not only more economically feasible and ideologically palatable, but in the shift from market-driven to conceptual-oriented design, all that was needed was something that could be photographed and disseminated through a magazine, however fictitious it was.

Like Sottsass's 'Superboxes', some of Archizoom Associati's products were subsequently produced. Progressive manufacturers, such as Poltronova and Gufram, picked up on the appeal objects like the 'Superonda' and 'Safari' sofas had for the growing youth market. Increasingly, however, these Pop products were themselves seen as problematic. The Marxist architectural historian Manfredo Tafuri (1989: 99) criticized Archizoom Associati and the associated Superstudio group as peddling an 'increasingly commercialized' form of irony, and by the 1970s these design objects were seen as an inadequate and too easily commodified critical response.

The crisis of Italian design and the complexity of its responses were most famously on display in the landmark 1972 MoMA exhibition 'Italy: The New Domestic Landscape: Achievements and Problems in Italian Design'. Curated by the Argentinean architect Emilio Ambasz, this was the most comprehensive survey of Italian design of the postwar period. Alongside the displays of design objects, from the mainstream elegance of Magistretti's 'Selene' to Sottsass's radical 'Superboxes', were eleven especially commissioned 'domestic environments'. Ambasz invited architects including Gae Aulenti, Gaetano Pesce, Superstudio and Sottsass to produce designs that ultimately demonstrated the degrees of contestation that were increasingly defining Italy's countercultural design movement.

Sottsass's 'environment' consisted of a series of interconnected grey fibreglass furnishing units. It epitomized the turn towards dematerialization in Italian design, influenced by larger movements in the international artistic avant-garde. In the catalogue, Sottsass (Ambasz 1972: 162) described how he wanted to make furniture 'from which we feel so detached, so disinterested, and so uninvolved that it is of absolutely no importance to us'. He also attended to the stage-set status of these objects:

> Given the time and conditions, and given the general views held by people as well, my pieces of furniture on view in this exhibition can be nothing more than prototypes, or perhaps even pre-prototypes, and thus, if you approach them, you realize that hardly anything really 'works' . . . These pieces of furniture, in fact, represent a series of ideas, and not a series of products to be put on the market this evening or tomorrow morning.

Ambasz's design brief explicitly advocated conceiving the environments as prototypes. This was not necessarily because he saw them as precursors to production, but because as an object type, he saw (Ambasz 1969) the prototype as best revealing the true nature of design. Increasingly, design was being understood more as a process of synthesis related to its surrounding environment rather than a fetishized formal solution. This overt attention to the prototype points to a shift in the Marxism that had defined much of the politics of Italy's left-wing architects. In the early 1970s it mirrored a larger idea that if architects wanted change, then they had to go further back in the design process than the superstructural level of designing commodities; change would only occur at the level of designing the processes of design and manufacture.

DESIGNING PRODUCTION, DESIGNING DESIGN

This was at its most explicit in an early 1970s project by the Marxist firebrand Mari. In 1974 Mari put on an exhibition entitled *Proposta per un'Autoprogettazione* (Proposal for a Self-Design) in Milan. It featured eighteen self-declared prototypes of furniture, including chairs, desks, a wardrobe and beds, all designed by Mari and produced by the Bolognese producer Simon International.

Even in the context of the exhibition, the emphasis was more on the process rather than the object. The catalogue was, in fact, a manual of photos and design drawings with a statement by Mari included in the front (2008: 1):

> A project for making easy-to-assemble furniture using rough boards and nails. An elementary technique to teach anyone to look at present production with a critical eye. (Anyone, apart from factories and traders, can use these designs to make them by themselves. The author hopes the idea will last into the future and asks those who build the furniture, and in particular, variations of it, to send photos to his studio.)

The connection between prototype and product was loosening; these designs would not be mass produced by professional manufacturers but handmade by amateurs in the domestic sphere. Furthermore, as Mari's rejection of 'factories and traders' suggests, this was not some project of benign do-it-yourself but participatory activism. In making the users put the furniture together themselves, Mari aimed to expose the mystification and inflated value of commodities.

For some radical designers, however, this controlled form of participation did not go far enough. In a series of *tecnica povera* (minimal technology) experiments conducted by the architect Riccardo Dalisi between 1971 and 1973 in Traiano, one of Naples's most impoverished quarters, the design process was itself reimagined. Dalisi's much-lauded project paralleled the *povera* movement in art, theatre and architecture. Influenced by the structural anthropology of Claude Lévi-Strauss (1972), advocates of *povera* proposed direct participation and the use of natural, or rather unmediated, materials in order to return to the unalienated condition of the 'savage mind'. Dalisi engaged in a game of behavioural primitivism in which he encouraged Neapolitan street children to design and make improvised, spontaneous furniture—these barely educated children were seen to be subjects who were as unconditioned by culture as possible. The chairs that resulted were the prototypes not for a new aesthetic or style but rather for a new design method based on play and participation.

Dalisi's experiments were taken up by Global Tools, the collective setup in 1973 that is seen to have marked the apotheosis and decline of Italian radical design. Set up in the offices of *Casabella*, then edited by radical architect Alessandro Mendini, Global Tools was populated by the leading lights of Italian radicalism, from Sottsass to Archizoom Associati, Superstudio and Gaetano Pesce. The group proposed a definition of tools as a form of communication, as media, as extensions of the body. Although Global Tools broke up three years later, it was their understanding of tools and design in general, clearly influenced by the writings of Marshall McLuhan (1964), that would later be taken up by the Memphis architects.

Although it was a decade of increasingly fragmented and disparate design activity, by the mid-1970s radical design was no longer about objects at all. This was a period of increasingly dystopian views, where nonmaking gave way, in its most nihilist and pessimistic form, to unmaking, to destruction. Mendini's 'Monumentino da Casa' (Little Household Monument), a laminate-covered wooden chair from 1974 produced by the experimental Cassina offshoot Braccio di Ferro was designed and made solely to be burnt and then featured on the cover of *Casabella*. The flat, photographic space of the magazine had become the loci of design activity in this period, serving to document the increasingly performative nature of radical design.

Mendini did get around to making objects again. In 1978 he joined Studio Alchymia, the Milanese gallery and studio set up by siblings Adriana and Alessandro Guerriero two years earlier. He was accompanied by Branzi, De Lucchi, Sottsass and several other protagonists of radical design. Branzi (1984: 141) described their 1979 'Bauhaus' collection as the first example of the New Handicrafts of the postindustrial landscape. As in all of postwar Italian design, there is no ideological distinction between artisanal and industrial making here: 'the prototype and the limited run make no pretence of being an alternative to mass-production, but treat it as a possible subsequent phase to the experiments in design permitted by the new handicrafts.'

However, to describe Alchymia's designs as prototypes was not strictly accurate. As Barbara Radice, journalist, Sottsass's partner and Memphis biographer, described (1993: 212), these one-off designs 'envisaged neither production nor commercial distribution.' However, while Mendini maintained the desire to keep distant from the mass market, De Lucchi and Sottsass saw this as the only viable arena of communication. This contributed to them breaking away from Alchymia to set up Memphis a year later.

Two design projects merit attention in the move from Alchymia to Memphis. First were Branzi and Sottsass's furniture designs for the Italian department store Croff Casa. With their bright but unpatterned surfaces, totemic yet recognizably furniture-like forms, their designs sat somewhere between the 'Superboxes' and Memphis. However, this step back towards the marketplace was disastrous. According to Radice (1985: 23), the department store sales assistants 'actually discouraged clients from buying the pieces'.

At least they got past the prototype stage. In 1979, while still with Alchymia, De Lucchi exhibited a series of painted wooden prototypes for small appliances that had been commissioned by the Italian domestic goods firm Girmi at the Milan *Triennale*. These toy-like, pastel-coloured forms were meant to signal a new aesthetic for domestic technologies. They were warmly received by the Italian press, and yet they were never put into production by Girmi, a belated reminder that prototypes do not always lead to products.

MAKING MEMPHIS, MARKETING MEMPHIS

Memphis seemed to have learnt from these experiences: conventionality in terms of production and dissemination did not guarantee market success. Accordingly, the roles of designers and manufacturers were renegotiated; if the latter could not be relied on to put these provocative imaginings into the marketplace, then their role had to be circumvented through the media.

Ernesto Gismondi, director of lighting company Artemide, was both one of Memphis's financial backers and its president. He was given no say in which objects went into production for the first Memphis collection, nor in the technologies or materials used. Instead, designs were discussed amongst the group at Sottsass's house and sent to the workshop of Renzo Brugola, a carpenter who had worked with Sottsass since the 1950s and who was also one of the Memphis partners, along with Brunella and Mario Godani, who owned the Arc '74 showroom (Rossi 2010).

From his Brianza workshop, Brugola coordinated production of the Memphis furniture, subcontracting local specialist workshops in the process. As Memphis progressed, the more it engaged with Italy's wealth of regionally based craft traditions. For the second 1982 collection, the Memphis architects designed domestic furnishings and accessories handmade by Murano's glass blowers, Vicenza's silversmiths, Carrara's marble manufacturers and Montelupo's ceramic manufacturers.

This network of integrated scales of production reflected the shape of Italian industry in the early 1980s. In the context of economic crisis, large industry was effectively stagnant. In its place was what the British magazine *Design* (Anon. 1983: 41) described 'as an anachronistic industrial structure; a network of family-run firms combines with a layer of craft-rich artisans to translate the often vague proposals of designers into prototypes and mass-produced goods.'

No construction drawings exist for the Memphis furniture. Instead, the architect and artisan relied on informal forms of visual and verbal communication. By now Brugola knew which thickness of materials Sottsass liked and his preference for rounded corners; Sottsass would give Brugola some sketches and just say 'arrangiarti!'—get on with it (Rossi 2010)! However, for all this reliance on Italy's continuing wealth of craft skills, any notion of this being some sort of 'craft revival' was denied by both critics and the architects themselves (Sudjic 1982: 42).

Instead, these were prototypes destined for industrial production. As Sottsass explained (Sudjic 1982: 42), 'they can all be produced by machines. Plastic laminate is made by a machine as are all the other elements.' However there was a problem with this desire for machine manufacture. As an exasperated Gismondi (Anon. 1989: 11) would later describe of Sottsass's *Carlton* room divider: 'The bookcase is built up of numerous pieces of plastic laminate glued onto wood, each piece being different from all the others. On no account can this be produced in series. There is no option other than doing it by hand.'

If more prototypes had been developed, then these problems could potentially have been ironed out. These prototype-as-products were partly due to the short time lag between the foundation of Memphis and its unveiling at the 1981 *Salone*, the most important date in the design calendar. The speed from concept to prototype and the provisionality of the objects also testifies to the inbuilt aesthetic obsolesce, or rather deliberate fashionability, of the objects, and increasingly, design in general, in the 1980s. It also ties in with another condition of these objects, one linked with the sheets of laminates that were plastered over every surface. These were produced by Abet Laminati, Italy's largest manufacturer of laminates, who had also financed Memphis and sponsored its catalogue. This continued their role as benefactor and beneficiary of radical design. Abet Laminati had sponsored 'Italy: The New Domestic Landscape' and provided the laminates for Sottsass's 'Superboxes'. By the early 1980s this relationship became more concrete in a series of Abet adverts that promoted their design connections. As with all marketing exercises, this was a mutually beneficial relationship; as producers of 'semi-finished' products (Castelli, Antonelli and Picchi 2007: 198), Abet could not participate on their own in the *Salone*. Instead, as they had done since the 1960s and before, they had to find design partners willing to design objects using their materials.

THE PROBLEM OF PROTOTYPES: ALESSI'S 'TEA AND COFFEE PIAZZA'

The postmodern prototype can therefore be understood principally as a publicity ploy. This is confirmed by one of the most well-known manifestations of Italian postmodernism: the 'Tea and Coffee Piazza' project. Instigated by Mendini, the project brought together designs by eleven different architects for the Italian firm Alessi. This was an example of the design editor phenomenon of designers that would flourish in the 1980s.

The services were available in sterling silver in limited editions of ninety-nine. There were also three prototypical 'proofs' of each service available in brass or silvered copper. Unlike with the Memphis objects, there was a considerable time lag between the inception and realization of these objects. While first dreamt up in 1979, the 'Tea and Coffee Piazza' services would not go into production until 1983, yet they made their first public appearance in an advert in *Domus* in 1981 under the headline 'L'Officina Alessi'. The advert featured drawings of prototypes for some of the tea and coffee pots by the architects involved, including Aldo Rossi, Robert Venturi, Denise Scott Brown and Mendini himself (Figure 2.4). According to the advert's lengthy copy (*L'Officina Alessi* 1981):

> Other prototypes, at this time, are being defined and will be reconsidered by the authors. Other studies, other preparatory sketches are in the course of being elaborated . . . From the designs of this group of architects will be made prototypes, or curiosities, or small productive series, or objects destined to enter into mass Alessi production.

The same advert was printed in *Casabella*, and prototypes of some of the services were shown in exhibitions in Germany, Switzerland and Italy from 1982 onwards. With such widespread marketing and such preeminence of the prototype, Alessi was surely confident of success. But the advert was really a piece of bravado—no one knew at that stage if all of the designs for the 'Piazzas' could even be made as prototypes, let alone be put into large-scale production.

The key to the story lies back in 1979. Alberto Alessi, the son of the firm's founder, was in charge of the project. He gave descriptions to the participating architects of what could and could not be done with stainless steel, the default Alessi material for Alessi production. They were offered the choice of designing for either small- or industrial-scale production, and all chose to work towards the latter. With sketches and design drawings beginning to arrive, the question of how to make the 'Piazzas' came to the fore. In Alberto's words (Gabra-Liddell 1994: 38–9):

> The time came to make a few prototypes, and that is when the problems started . . . almost none of the projects had the necessary characteristics for series production, and the option of small-scale artisan production included

Figure 2.4   Alessandro Mendini, design for the *Tea & Coffee Piazza* project, Alessi, electro-plated silver, 1983. © Aldo Ballo, Museo Alessi.

by myself in the brief with great bravery and foolhardiness, was in actual fact very difficult to put into practice at Alessi. All our excellent mechanics and model makers, the only people able to work on a small-scale series, were already involved with the construction of the moulds and the prototypes necessary to the ranges already in production.

Over the next couple of years Alberto had a few prototypes covertly made in the Alessi workshop; the other members of the family were either unconvinced or never even told about the project. Come 1982 Alberto was under pressure from Mendini to provide closure, and he handed production over to several artisans in the Milanese hinterland. He had to pay for the first silver prototypes out of his own pocket—such was his concern that his family would not look too favourably on the idea (Gabra-Liddell 1994: 39).

Even once the prototypes were made, Alberto's woes were not over (Gabra-Liddell 1994: 39): 'I realised . . . that it was one thing making the prototypes, and another selling these objects, which always resulted in being more exciting from the expressive point of view, but were scarcely functional and extremely expensive.' The preemptive exhibitions in Europe in 1982 became just the first step in a large-scale, international publicity campaign that deliberately sought out museums, galleries and private collectors—the only possible buyers for these exorbitantly priced objects.

So the decision to make small-scale, silver objects was not desired from the outset. Just like the Memphis furniture, despite the wishes of the manufacturer and even the architects involved, Alessi's 'Tea and Coffee Piazzas' could not be mass produced, certainly not at an accessible price. Instead, they were reliant on and designed in mind with the ongoing wealth of artisans willing and able to interpret architects' ideas into reality, as well as innovative manufacturers willing to invest time and money into design research.

CONCLUSION

From the 'Superleggera' to the 'Tea and Coffee Piazzas', this chapter has demonstrated the centrality of the prototype to the story of postwar Italian design. Taken together, it is clear that throughout this period, from 1945 to the early 1980s, the prototype was caught up in Italian design's ambiguous relationship with postwar modernity. At first certain of a future of industrial production, in the 1950s, architects, such as Ponti and the Castiglioni brothers, were designing objects suited for a mass system of production and consumption that did not exist. In the crisis of consumerist values in the mid-1960s Italy's architects lost their faith in both this certainty and any clear-cut future at all. By the 1980s Sottsass and his band of Memphis architects were designing objects that could not be produced or consumed on a large-scale. Increasingly, however, this did not matter; once photographed and disseminated, the prototype had performed its function as a vehicle for communication, and the distinction between prototype and product had therefore collapsed.

Throughout, one thing remained a constant about the prototype—its position at the centre of an ongoing discourse between design, craft and industry in postwar Italy, one that shows up the strength and the cracks of this vital tripartite relationship.

FURTHER READING

Ambasz, E. (1969), 'The Formulation of a Design Discourse', *Perspecta*, 12: 57–70.

Ambasz, E. (ed.) (1972), 'Italy: New Domestic Landscape: Achievements and Problems in Italian Design', New York: MoMA in collaboration with Centro Di, Florence.

Anon., (1983), 'Paragon and Paradox', *Design*, September, 417, 41.

Anon., (1989), *Memphis, 1981–1988*, Groningen: Groninger Museum.

Anon., (1991), *Memphis: La Collection Karl Lagerfeld*, Monte Carlo: Sotheby's.

Branzi, A. (1984), *The Hot House: Italian New Wave Design*, London: Thames and Hudson.

Castelli, G., Antonelli, P., and Picchi, F. (eds) (2007), *La Fabbrica del Design: Conversazioni con i protagonisti del Design Italiano*, Milan: Skira.

Gabra-Liddell, M. (1994), *Alessi: Design Factory*, Chichester: Academy Editions.

Lévi-Strauss, C. (1972), *The Savage Mind*, 3rd edn, London: Weidenfeld and Nicolson.

L'Officina Alessi (1981), *Domus*, June, 618.

Magistretti, V., Giacomoni, S., and Marcolli, A. (1988), *Designer Italiani*, Milan: Idealibri, 187, trans. K. Singleton in Pasca, V. (1991), *Vico Magistretti: Elegance and Innovation in Postwar Italian Design*, London: Thames and Hudson, 49.

Mari, E. (1981), *Dov'è l'Artigiano*, Florence: Fortezz da Basso.

Mari, E. (2008), *Autoprogettazione?* Mantua: Corraini.

McLuhan, M. (1964), *Understanding Media: The Extensions of Man*, London: Routledge and Kegan Paul.

Nelson, G. (1983), 'A Tourist's Guide to MEMPHIS', *Interior Design*, 54: 214–21.

Pasca, V. (1991), *Vico Magistretti: Elegance and Innovation in Postwar Italian Design*, trans. K. Singleton, London: Thames and Hudson.

Ponti, G. (1952), 'Senza Aggettivi', *Domus*, March, 268, 1.

Pye, D. (1968), *The Nature and Art of Workmanship*, London: Cambridge University Press.

Radice, B. (1985), *Memphis: Research, Experiences, Results, Failures and Successes of New Design*, trans. P. Blanchard, London: Thames and Hudson.

Radice, B. (1993), *Ettore Sottsass: A Critical Biography*, London: Thames and Hudson.

Rossi, C. (2010), 'Crafting Modern Design in Italy, From Post-War to Postmodernism', PhD thesis, History of Design department, RCA/Victoria & Albert Museum, London.

Sparke, P. (1990), 'A Home for Everybody?: Design, Ideology and the Culture of the Home in Italy, 1945–1972', in Z. G. Barański and R. Lumley (eds), *Culture and Conflict in Postwar Italy: Essays on Mass and Popular Culture*, Houndsmill: Macmillan, 225–41.

Sudjic, D. (1982), 'Sottsass and Co.', *Crafts*, November/December, 59, 42.

Tafuri, M. (1989), *History of Italian Architecture: 1944–1985*, trans. J. Levine, Cambridge, MA: MIT Press.

ACKNOWLEDGEMENTS

My thanks in particular to Dr Glenn Adamson and Dr Louise Valentine and to Renzo Brugola and the archives of Cassina, Michele De Lucchi and Ettore Sottsass.

3 THE IMAGINATIVE USE OF FICTIONAL BIO-PROTOTYPES

FRASER BRUCE AND SEATON BAXTER

Most people now acknowledge that we live in a world of serious multiple crises, all of which appear to culminate in one large, interconnected turbulent crisis verging, for some, on chaos. The list of problems seems endless: climate change, pollution and loss of biodiversity, social inequality and injustice, organized crime, violence and corruption of anything from food systems to politics. From an ecological perspective, natural environments are under increasing pressure; as the world's population continues to grow, it increases the already high resource consumption of Western developed countries, and these environments are now also under pressure by the rapidly expanding economies of China and India, for example. These problems have come about, in part, from our fragmented view of the world and hence our inability to foresee the interconnections and to consider the consequences of our individual actions. Designers contribute to this fragmented critical situation where, through their association with business, commerce and industry, they have created new products, processes and performances with no overview and understanding of the whole system. As Homer-Dixon (2000) has pointed out, our technological ingenuity continues to add to the complexity of the world, thereby giving rise to new, unpredictable emergent situations, some of which may be harmful to life. Our ingenuity is unlikely to keep pace with increasing complexity. Unfortunately, however, with these new problems, we have no precedent from which to learn; these problems are unbelievably complex (or wicked) and will require a different mix of problem-solving techniques and more teamwork of a multidisciplinary nature. They consist of what Donald Rumsfeld has referred to as 'unknown unknowns, the things we don't know we don't know'.[1] The problems that we will now have to confront will be characterized by the following:

1. They will be unique, that is, we have no precedent to learn from.
2. They will all be part of a large-scale interconnected web, scale-linked at all system levels.

3. They will centre around living systems—biological, ecological and sociological interactions.
4. They will necessitate the interlocking of many knowledge domains.
5. They will be extremely complex (or wicked).

We refer to problems with these characteristics as *Alien Problems*. The questions for us in this chapter are: How can designers learn to handle problems of this nature, and can the technique of prototyping contribute to this learning experience? As Paul Hawkins remarks in Leonardo DiCaprio's film *The 11th Hour*, 'the great thing about being in our present predicament is that we will have to re-imagine everything'.[2]

All designers are generally recognized as problem-solvers, but if they are to enter the domain of these new problems (Aliens), they will have to change their mindsets and adjust their approaches and techniques accordingly. The philosopher Sir Karl Popper remarked that all of life involves problem-solving. On a daily basis, everyone confronts and solves problems in both their personal and working lives all the time. A problem, in its most general sense, can be defined as a discrepancy between an existing situation and an alternative desired state of affairs. In other words, all problems have a similar structure made up of certain characteristics: (*a*) a particular situation or condition (*The Given State*), (*b*) a desired state to be reached (*The Goal State*) and (*c*) no clear or obvious way to change the state (*The Obstacles*). Problems can also be classified as being either well structured or ill structured. For instance, some problems are simple and well-structured and can have many possible solutions that are either right or wrong. More complicated problems may require several steps and iterations to resolve them (i.e. broken down into smaller pieces with each piece being solved independently). Most of these kinds of problems are amenable to conventional problem-solving methods. In contrast, however, many real-world problems are ill structured and are often referred to as 'wicked' problems' (Rittel and Webber 1973). According to Rittel and Webber, wicked problems emerge from socially complex issues and have ten unique characteristics that differentiate them from other types of problems (1973: 161–7):

1. 'There is no definitive formulation of a wicked problem.'
2. 'Wicked problems have no stopping rule.'
3. 'Solutions to wicked problems are not true or false, but good or bad.'
4. 'There is no immediate and no ultimate test of a solution to a wicked problem.'
5. 'Every solution to a wicked problem is a "one-shot operation" because there is no opportunity to learn by trial and error, every attempt counts significantly.'

6. 'Wicked problems do not have an enumerable (or an exhaustively describable) set of potential solutions, nor is there a well-described set of permissible operations that may be incorporated into the plan.'
7. 'Every wicked problem is essentially unique.'
8. 'Every wicked problem can be considered to be a symptom of another problem.'
9. 'The existence of a discrepancy representing a wicked problem can be explained in numerous ways.'
10. 'The planner has no right to be wrong.'

Complex problems of this nature are not amenable to resolution through conventional approaches and so will require more original (novel) ways to reach a desired goal state. A change of strategy from routine to creative will be required (Henry 1991). The Creative Problem-Solving (CPS) process, unlike ordinary problem-solving, always involves creativity,[3] and it is about seeing problems differently and stimulating imaginative new ideas in ways that are useful and appropriate to others. As Brown, Harris and Russell (2010: 4) have remarked:

> the task is therefore to draw on all our intellectual resources, valuing the contributions of all the academic disciplines as well as other ways in which we construct our knowledge. And that brings the challenge of developing open transdisciplinary modes of inquiry capable of meeting the needs of the individual, the community, the specialist traditions, and influential organizations, and allows for a holistic leap of the imagination.

The word imagination comes from the Latin word *imaginari*, meaning 'faculty of the mind which forms and manipulates images'.[4] So, in its broadest sense, imagination can be described as thought processes which facilitate the creation of mental images of things that we can neither see nor sense in reality. By detaching ourselves from reality through a variety of ways, such as pretend play, fantasy, make-believe and daydreaming, we provide not only meaning and purpose to experiences and understanding of knowledge but we also enjoy freedom to develop new ways of seeing the world and to envisage situations beyond what we currently know. Albert Einstein usefully captured the essence of imagination when he said: 'while knowledge defines all we currently know and understand, imagination points to all we might yet discover and create' (Clark 1984: 201). While imaginative thought is closely associated with the act of discovery and the ability to create, it also has strong interrelationships with problem-solving and innovation (i.e. the goal-orientated process for developing and successfully exploiting new ideas). Designing is often portrayed as the process that covers the whole spectrum of actions, but we believe that design tends to focus on the part that links creativity and innovation. Design is part of the process which uses a variety of tools and methods, of which prototyping is now a well-established technique.

PROTOTYPES, CONVENTIONAL AND UNCONVENTIONAL

In 1978 James G. Miller proposed and elaborated on a general living systems theory in which he analysed the structure and process of a hierarchy of seven levels of living systems and used this to explore the similarities and differences across these levels. The evidence was presented in a way which allowed comparisons of systems at two or more levels, and he demonstrated the notion of scale-linking. The seven levels of living systems from the smallest to the largest are: (1) the cell, (2) the organ, (3) the organism, (4) the group, (5) the organization, (6) the society and (7) the supranational system. Throughout this chapter, we refer to these levels using this numbered system with the intention of locating prototypes and systems at different levels.

In conventional prototyping, the prototype is both an activity *and* an artefact (Schrage, in this volume) where the artefact or potential artefact is always embedded within the activity. The activity of prototyping is usually an intentional, problem-solving activity that culminates in some form of artefact. An individual or a team of individuals may perform prototyping. In both cases, there is a requirement for imagination, intelligence and skills in resolving a technical problem. The technical problem, which usually deals with inanimate objects, can also be located at the lower levels (1–3) of Miller's Hierarchy. When a team is engaged in prototyping, this tends to raise the problem to higher levels (4–5) of Miller's Hierarchy. Where the problem is purely technical, the knowledge and skills required to solve it will depend on its degree of complication because, in most cases, the technical problem deals with inanimate (or nonliving) objects. The social problem, now involving team members, clients and so on, is always complex because it now involves the actions of living systems. Hence, bringing the two together, the technical problem and its resolution (by a team) is always complex (or wicked) and higher up on Miller's Hierarchy of Living Systems. Clearly, we need to understand these differences in order to manage the problem situation through the activity of prototyping. In relation to the characteristics of our Alien Problems, it looks as if conventional prototyping may well help us to confront one or two characteristics. The difficulty is that conventional prototyping is unlikely to play a major role in confronting all the characteristics of Alien Problems. Interestingly, however, there is an unconventional method of prototyping recently described by Johnson (2011) as *Science Fiction Prototyping*, which might serve our purposes better. Here, Johnson suggests that, although fictional prototypes have been used predominantly for entertainment purposes in the form of fictional comic book characters or superheroes, such as Superman and Batman, the true value of Science Fiction (SF) Prototyping is that it is capable of being applied to real-world scenarios. In these settings, he suggests we can use personas and scenarios, movies, stories and comics as tools to envision the future and devise new products, services and systems. So it is possible that fictional (or unconventional) prototyping can be used to stimulate the imagination to tackle Alien Problems. Regardless of whether prototyping is conventional or unconventional, in the activity associated with the technique, *play* will become an important component of collective problem-solving. Indeed, it is generally accepted that play is imaginative and often forms a central component of creative behaviour. Michael Schrage, one of the world's most innovative thought leaders on business innovation, has distinguished frivolous play from what he calls 'serious play':

> Serious play is not an oxymoron; it is the essence of innovation . . . It means innovation requires improvisation. It means innovation isn't about rigorously following 'the rules of the game', but about rigorously challenging and revising them. It means innovation is less the product of how innovators think than a by-product of how they behave. Serious play is about innovative behavior . . . The essence of serious play is the challenge and thrill of confronting uncertainties. Whether uncertainties are obstacles or allies depends on how you play. The challenge of converting uncertainty into manageable risks or opportunities explains why serious play is often the most rational behavior for innovators. (2000: 1–2)

At an operational level, Schrage also emphasizes the importance of prototyping as a play-based approach to learning that can be used as a mechanism to help build, support and maintain team cohesion within organizations, stating that: 'the notion that innovative teams generate innovative prototypes is giving way to a recognition that innovative prototypes are the focus for generating innovative teams' (2006: 202). The use of unconventional methods of prototyping now expands the range of problems to which prototyping can be applied.

PROTOTYPING AND TEAM-WORKING

Like Michael Schrage, Watkins (2003) recognizes the importance of team-working for understanding the link between creativity and innovation. However,

Table 3.1 The paradoxical characteristics of the creative group.

Beginners Mind	A team needs fresh, inexperienced perspectives as well as skilled expertise. Bringing in outsiders is often a useful way to provide the necessary balance of perspective.	Experience
Freedom	Your team must work well within the confines of real business needs—and in alignment with your company's strategy. But it also needs latitude—some degree of freedom to determine how it will achieve the strategy and address the business needs.	Discipline
Playfulness	Creativity thrives on playfulness, but business must be conducted professionally. Provide time and space for play, but clarify the appropriate times and places.	Professionalism
Improvisation	Plan your project carefully, but remember that projects do not always go as planned. Encourage team members to look for ways to turn unexpected events into opportunities. Keep plans flexible enough to incorporate new or improved ideas.	Planning

Source: Watkins (2003: 85).

he also highlights the contradictory tendencies in thought and action that exist side by side and refers to them as the paradoxical characteristics of creative groups (Table 3.1). While imagination and playfulness are central to Watkins's thinking, he clearly embeds them within several other key aspects of the creative group. This reminds us that playfulness and imagination are not the sole characteristics of the whole problem-solving process. For example, nearing the end of the design process, clear trade-offs and design decisions are necessary in order to arrive at a final solution.

Furthermore, in order to successfully design new products, services and systems in today's complex and turbulent market environments, Buchenau and Fulton Suri (2000: 425) also recognize the importance of multidisciplinary collaborations, stating that: 'Multiple disciplines are needed to solve the design problems of today—eg interaction design, industrial design, designers of environments, human factors specialists, mechanical and electrical engineers. Each discipline brings a unique understanding of the issues at hand and an individual approach to solving them.' They also acknowledge that prototypes and prototyping methods help teams share information and create common goals, saying that:

> To work effectively as a design team it is important to develop a common vision of what the team is trying to bring into being. Therefore, it is a powerful asset to have tools and techniques which create a shared experience, providing a foundation for a common point of view . . . The tools we use to design, such as prototypes, influence the way we think. Solutions, and probably even imagination, are inspired and limited by the prototyping tools we have at our disposal. (Buchenau and Fulton Suri 2000: 425)

Team-based unconventional prototyping is therefore a strong contender for exploring the full range of Alien Problems.

ALIEN PROBLEMS AND UNCONVENTIONAL PROTOTYPING

Although Johnson's SF prototyping is exciting and a potentially appropriate tool to explore Alien Problems, in our opinion, it is not yet a common approach used in design practice. There are, however, early examples of the use of fictional prototypes that we have experienced over a number of years even though these have not necessarily been applied to the resolution of Alien Problems. We now review each of these independent case studies with the intention of examining them in the light of the five characteristics of Alien Problems already stated. In addition, even where Johnson (2011) uses fictional prototypes of a biological nature, he is not necessarily using them in order to emphasize the importance of living systems knowledge into the prototyping activity. We refer to the intentional use of living systems prototypes as *Bio-Prototypes*. In the remainder of this chapter, we will set the context and background for each of the independent case studies, briefly describing the protocol, the outcomes and conclusions. Finally, we present some reflections on the use of Bio-Prototypes when tackling Alien Problems.

BIO-PROTOTYPES (CASE STUDIES I AND 2)

In 1982 one of us (SB) was involved in conducting an informal evening workshop as an adjunct to a scientific conference on the issue of farm animal welfare (Case Study 1). The conference brought together renowned animal scientists and designers. One of the problems confronted then, and one still common today, was the lack of collaboration or even serious conversations between disciplines that were needed in order to solve these complex animal-related problems. The workshop was designed to display and acknowledge the disciplinary knowledge and skills of the individual participants and to encourage transdisciplinary appreciation and understanding of their apparently individual positions. The participants were divided into groups of mixed scientists and designers. They were confronted with the following problem now known as the '*Imaginary Menagerie*'. The groups were given a coloured image (Bio-Prototype) of a 'Rabbuck' in its natural habitat. Though it was entirely the imaginative creation of paleogeographer Dougal Dixon, this composite creature, part rabbit and part buck (or *alien*), was originally conceived by Dixon as a potentially distant species (Dixon 1981: 38–9). The groups were asked in a sequence of over three to four hours to tackle the following 'design' problems and to report back at an informal plenary session later that night. The protocol was as follows:

1. Design the animal's anatomical, physiological, respiratory and reproductive systems—its biology (Miller's levels 1–3).
2. Describe the animal's behaviour in terms of food gathering, mating and so on—its ecology (Miller's levels 3 and 4).
3. Decide which attributes in the way of products or processes the animal might have which were worth acquiring for human consumption through domestication (includes Miller's levels 5 and 6).
4. Design the method of domestication and handling and all the facilities you would require to acquire these products (includes Miller's levels 5 and 6).
5. Design a marketing strategy for these products (includes Miller's level 7).

In 2008 the '*Imaginary Menagerie*' was again used in a one-day pilot workshop with a cohort of novice undergraduate students studying product design and interaction design at The University of Dundee (Case Study 2). The protocol for this workshop was identical to that outlined above in the 1982 version. However, there was one small change to the existing exercise: the eight groups were each given an 'extreme' version of a Bio-Prototype taken from *Flanimals*, a children's book by author Ricky Gervais (2007). The main objective was again to see how groups of participants (young designers in this case) would react to such an Alien Problem.

In both case studies, the protocol was impossible to complete in any detail in the time available. However, the exercise was not about the solutions but rather how the groups would tackle the problems operationally and socially. From participant feedback, the workshops were generally regarded as a useful and challenging experience, especially with regard to breaking down potential barriers and building new relationships between actors. Some interesting observations have emerged from these two case studies which are useful and appropriate to our early discussions on 'wicked' and Alien Problems. Firstly, where groups had a strong related knowledge base, for example domestic animal science (Case Study 1), they had no difficulty making a start at attempting to solve the Alien Problem. On the other hand, the novice design students (Case Study 2) lacked any related or extensive knowledge and therefore had difficulties finding an appropriate starting point (The Given State). In addition, the students' lack of understanding and an appropriate vocabulary meant a poor appreciation of the problems. Secondly, the maturity of the group influenced their ability to retain a serious approach to the problem, even when things got difficult and more complex (moved to higher levels of Miller's hierarchy). In Case Study 1, all participants were mature, knowledgeable and interested in tackling the problems. The students, however, found it difficult to even start solving the problem, and when the task got difficult, it was too easy for them to slide from 'serious play' (Schrage 2000) to 'frivolous play' and to defend this action by ridiculing the unreal nature of the problem. This then led to a lack of interest and demotivation. Finally, it was apparent that individuals in groups generally cooperated, but only in a partial manner. In Case Study 1, because the problem sequence favoured scientists to lead in the early stages of the exercise and designers in the latter stages, this division of the participants into disciplines tended to be reinforced. In Case Study 2, there was no clear disciplinary division between the students, and any individual differences were more about lack of motivation rather than a division of knowledge. However, cooperation appeared more satisfactory in the informal learning that took place in groups where individuals were more comfortable in the presence of one another. This was obvious in the subsequent research days of the conference (Case Study 1). Unfortunately, the knowledge base, skills and maturity of the student groups (Case Study 2) were too similar, and this provided little room for more expansive thinking (imagining). It was also hard for some students to accept that there were no ulterior standard assessment motives in such a weird exercise. The students' anxiety about this appeared to inhibit their open pursuit of answers.

It is also clear, however, that the environment in which these exercises were conducted was important. For instance, the students needed to be constantly reassured that they were working on an important—albeit unreal—problem for which there was no single correct answer, no means of evaluating their answer and hence no sense of failure (Rittel and Webber 1973). This kind of exercise is an 'adventure' rather than a test. For instance, Coelho reminds us about risk when he says: 'The boat is safest when it is in port. But that's not what boats were built for' (2007: 94).

BIO-PROTOTYPES (CASE STUDY 3)

In 2005 the Bio-Prototype Rabbuck was again introduced into a problem situation, but this time within a larger exercise with MSc Holistic Science students at Schumacher College. The 'Island Project' (Irwin, Kossoff and Baxter 2008) as it was known, required participants to work in groups to design in seven days an imaginary, evolving society on an island that would span a period of nearly 500 years. The models of the islands, themselves Bio-Prototypes (Miller's level 6), were simulations of Azorean Islands. The Bio-Prototype Rabbuck (Miller's level 3) was one of two alien species located on the islands, but in this case, the Rabbuck was presented as part of a wider ecological problem in a larger evolving space/ time context. The participants consisted of two self-selecting groups of seven students, all of whom had already participated in the early part of the MSc in Holistic Science. Participant evaluation indicated that the students found the exercise difficult but stimulating, engrossing and deeply thought-provoking. It was evident that the group that immersed itself more in the exercise gained more from it. The focus on the Rabbuck tended not to be at the design level featured in Case Study 1 but required the participants to place this Bio-Prototype in the larger context of the bio-prototypical ecological system of the islands. In addition, Case Study 3 required the participants to look at the coevolution of a human society and the nonhuman living system, which included the Rabbuck. For example, the direct association of the Rabbuck and humans required careful consideration of issues such as conservation, hunting, domestication and even the evolution of rituals. In Case Study 3, all participants knew each other well and were familiar with each other's skills, knowledge, experiences and idiosyncrasies. In addition, they had all been subjected to a new but common learning experience called holistic science. The following points from Case Study 3 are of interest. Firstly, it appears that groups with wide-ranging experiences and good preparatory reading settle more quickly into complex problem-solving. Secondly, group dynamics, especially the method of leadership, has significant effects. Indeed, initial conditions at the beginning of the exercise are important. For example, in one group, a student of business management emerged as the leader and adopted a bureaucratic, rule-bound approach to the exercise. In contrast, the second group adopted a democratic, participatory approach to the learning experience. Interestingly, the more bureaucratic group was the older group, but here maturity may well have inhibited a more open approach to the problem. On this occasion, there were no doubts in the minds of all participants that the problem itself was relevant. Finally, groups who play best, let go of their existing inhibitions and immerse themselves in the real and virtual experiences gain most from the experience. They become almost childlike in their actions and playfulness.

REFLECTIONS ON THE USE OF BIO-PROTOTYPES

In all three case studies, we found that fictional Bio-Prototypes were valuable in creating a learning environment for design problems for which there was no prior knowledge. In Case Study 3, the use of Bio-Prototypes at different scale-linked systems levels also proved valuable in reinforcing the idea of systems relationships and interconnections. Case Study 2 demonstrated that groups of immature participants have difficulties dealing with Bio-Prototypes of an extreme nature. This of course may also be true of more mature groups, but we have no experience of this. How extreme can a fictional prototype be and still contribute to a useful exercise is an interesting question. We propose that the studies described above involved a form of fictional, unconventional prototyping similar to that discussed by Johnson (2011), and as a consequence, the studies are relevant to technical, ecological and social problem-solving, as well as stimulating the imagination when tackling Alien Problems. We therefore conclude with the following fifteen thoughts based on what we have learned from these exercises about Alien Problems and problem-solving. These thoughts should also be usefully read in association with the ten characteristics of wicked problems outlined earlier in this chapter:

1. Alien Problems are a particular kind of complex problem which require a high degree of imagining.
2. The knowledge base for tackling them is often tenuous or nonexistent; they are unique.
3. They can have difficult starting points because they are unbelievably complex (or wicked).
4. They are usually best tackled by groups or teams, as more skills and knowledge domains can lead to better informed decisions and possible resolutions.
5. Groups or teams are better when they are transdisciplinary because this increases the possibility of accessing some appropriate starting knowledge.
6. Participants with wide experience and wide reading increase the prospects of finding an early start and tend to maintain impetus.
7. Struggling with problems of this nature is like competing in a rodeo—the atmosphere can be turbulent, unpredictable, even unreal and dangerous. This is a domain where the balance between executing intentional design tactics is subordinated to coping with emergence.
8. Where the complexity of the problem is overwhelming and inhibits further progress, changing the project to a complicated problem may be a short-term strategy. In other words, you tame the beast by making the problem complicated rather than complex and return to the fray when you feel better prepared.

9. Knowing a wider context for the problem increases its complexity but often provides clues to finding an appropriate starting point.
10. Play is an essential strategy for tackling this kind of problem and serious play for staying with it.
11. The use of imagination is an essential component of serious play.
12. The working environment for play should be conducive to playfulness.
13. Complex problems are complex because of relationships, especially those embracing living beings—that is the hassle factor of working with others.
14. Failure is not an outcome of this kind of problem, as Coelho says: 'Only one thing makes a dream impossible,—the fear of failure' (2007: 8).
15. Working on Alien Problems of this kind is not a task but an adventure.

NOTES

1. Donald Rumsfeld, press conference, NATO, Brussels, 2 June 2002, http://www.defense.gov/transcripts/transcript.aspx?transcriptid=3490.
2. Leila Connors and Nadia Conners (dir.), *The 11th Hour*, film, 95 minutes (Warner Independent Pictures, 2007).
3. According to Henry (1991: 3), 'creativity is about the quality of originality that leads to new ways of seeing and novel ideas. It is a thinking process associated with imagination, insight, invention, innovation, ingenuity, inspiration and illumination. However, creativity is not just about novelty: for an idea to be truly creative it must also be appropriate and useful.'
4. 'Imagination image,' Online Etymology Dictionary, http://www.etymonline.com/index.php?search=Imagination+image.

FURTHER READING

Brown, V. A., Harris, J. A., and Russell, J. Y. (2010), *Tackling Wicked Problems through the Transdisciplinary Imagination*, London: Earthscan.

Buchenau, M., and Fulton Suri, J. (2000), 'Experience Prototyping', in B. Boyarski and W. A. Kellog (eds), *Proceedings of the Conference on Designing Interactive Systems: Processes, Practices, Methods, Techniques*, New York: ACM Press.

Clark, R. W. (1984), *Einstein: The Life and Times*, New York: Avon Books.

Coelho, P. (2007), *Life: Selected Quotations*, London: HarperCollins.

Dixon, D. (1981), *After Man: A Zoology of the Future*, London: Granada.

Gervais, R., and Steen, R. (2007), *Flanimals: The Day of the Bletchling*, London: Faber Children's Books.

Henry, J. (1991), *Creative Management*, London: Sage.

Homer-Dixon, T. (2000), *The Ingenuity Gap*, London: Jonathan Cape.

Irwin, T., Kossoff, G., and Baxter, S. (2008), 'Island: A Unique Group Learning Experience in Long-view Trans-disciplinary Designing', in N. Houghton (ed.), *Enhancing Curricula: Using Research and Enquiry to Inform Student Learning in the Disciplines*, London: The Centre for Learning and Teaching in Art and Design, 443–55.

Johnson, B. D. (2011), *Science Fiction Prototyping: Designing the Future with Science Fiction*, San Rafael, CA: Morgan & Claypool.

Miller, J. G. (1978), *Living Systems*, New York: McGraw-Hill.

Rittel, H., and Webber, M. (1973), 'Dilemmas in a General Theory of Planning', *Policy Sciences*, 4: 155–69.

Schrage, M. (2000), *Serious Play: How the World's Best Companies Simulate to Innovate*, Boston: Harvard Business School Press.

Schrage, M. (2006), 'Cultures of Prototyping', in T. Winograd (ed.), *Bringing Science to Software*, New York: ACM Press, http://hci.stanford.edu/publications/bds/10-Schrage.pdf, accessed 12 December 2012.

Watkins, M. (2003), *Managing for Creativity and Innovation*, Boston: Harvard Business School Press, 85.

ACKNOWLEDGEMENTS

The authors gratefully acknowledge the contributions of Terry Irwin, Gideon Kossoff and Sean Kingsley for aspects of this work. We would also like to thank all the participants along the way.

4 PROTOTYPING FOR THE DESIGN SPACES OF THE FUTURE

ELIZABETH B.-N. SANDERS

OVERVIEW

Prototypes have been used throughout design history as a means of bringing ideas to life before the ideas are built or manufactured. But just as design today is undergoing radical change, so too are prototypes and the activity of prototyping. Prototyping is becoming a participatory activity. I propose a new view on prototyping and describe how we can use prototyping to help us not only give shape to but also make sense of the future. It is only through collective thinking and acting that we will be able to use design to help address the social and cultural issues we face today. We know how prototypes are used to help us shape the future, but what does it mean to use prototyping to make sense of the future?

THE CONTEXT OF DESIGN IS CHANGING

Four manifestations of change can be seen today in design: a shift in the focus of design, the rise of creative activities for nondesigners, the interest by business people in design-thinking and the obsession with cocreation by all kinds of people. These manifestations of change reveal the need for new tools, methods and mindsets to support collective forms of creativity.

The shift in the focus of design is described in Figure 4.1 and shows how the design domains are in the midst of a radical transformation. Design has been, until recently, primarily concerned with the making of 'stuff'. The traditional fields of design education are characterized by the type of stuff that designers learn to make (e.g. industrial designers make products and architects make buildings). Prototypes made during the traditional design process represent objects, such as possible future products, spaces or buildings. The languages that designers learn in school are specialized for the creating of these types of objects. For example, traditional design embodiments for making stuff include sketches, drawings, prototypes and models.

Design practice is now moving from a focus on the making of stuff to a focus on making stuff for people in the context of their lives. The emerging design

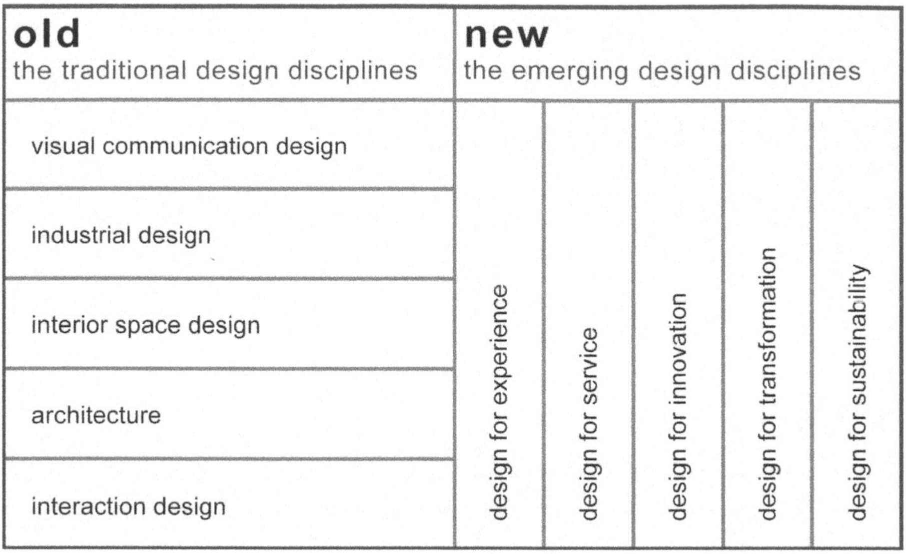

old the traditional design disciplines	new the emerging design disciplines				
visual communication design	design for experience	design for service	design for innovation	design for transformation	design for sustainability
industrial design					
interior space design					
architecture					
interaction design					

Figure 4.1   Old and New Design Domains. The design domains are transforming from a focus on the objects of design (old) to a focus on the purpose of design (new). Credit: Elizabeth B.-N. Sanders.

domains on the right side of Figure 4.1 are focused on intent, or the purpose of design—for example, design for the purpose of serving or healing or transforming. Thus, in these new design domains, there is, the need for telling and enacting stories—that is, stories about how people will live and how they wish they could live in the future. There is the need for alternative forms of conceptualization and embodiment beyond stuff. Alternative embodiments for describing and enacting experience include stories, future scenarios, narratives, performance art, documentaries and timelines of experience.

Another manifestation of change in design is the increase in the number of people seeking creative activities. There is now the growing recognition that all people are creative. This can be seen in the growth of the DIY (do-it-yourself) industry and the resurgence of crafting at all levels. The rise of social networks and other means of online sharing have contributed widely to this phenomenon; www.etsy.com is a good example. The rise of creative activity-seeking by nondesigners may also be a reaction against the overemphasis on consumption that marks much of the world's people today. Or perhaps it is a seeking for the 'convivial tools' that Illich (1973) described over forty years ago. We are finally learning that we need to balance consumptive and creative opportunities for everyone.

A third manifestation of change is the recent interest and enthusiasm in what is called 'design thinking'. The phenomenon is particularly popular in the business community (Martin 2009). Design thinking is already of such interest that business schools within universities around the world are attempting to revamp their curricula to meet the needs of business students who do not want to play the business as usual game.

Concomitant with the rise in creativity that we see from everyday people and the interest from the business community in design thinking is the recent obsession with cocreation (Sanders and Simons 2009) at all stages of the design development process. This change brings with it the need for new forms and means of supporting and inspiring collective creativity—that is, creativity shared by people.

DESIGN IS CHANGING

The manifestations of change that we see in the contextual landscape of design have resulted in a number of shifts in how designing is done today. The shifts can be seen in where it is happening, when it is happening and who is involved.

WHERE IS IT TAKING PLACE?

In the past, design took place in the studio, and design research took place in the laboratory or in the field (i.e. the context of use). Today design and research occur anywhere designers and researchers meet. The meeting places are just as likely to be online groups as they are to be shared offices or coffee shops. Designing takes place out in the world. This extends the possibilities for using experiential and environmental contexts for inspiration and imagination.

WHEN IS IT HAPPENING?

Ten to fifteen years ago design research played a strong role in the evaluation of design ideas and concepts. Since then, design and research activities have been moving progressively towards the front end of the design process. Today most design research firms are playing in (or attempting to play in) the arena of the fuzzy front end, or the predesign phase in the design development process. It is here that the design and research activities focus on exploring the landscape of opportunities in order to determine what to design and why. We are also learning that it is the place to determine what *not* to design and why not.

WHO IS INVOLVED?

Design has become an increasingly collaborative activity. This is particularly true in the fuzzy front end where participation from people in all disciplines is now recognized as being important. Most of them are not trained in design or design research, and they come with their own disciplinary tools, methods and mindsets. The challenges we face today are large and complex. Physical manifestations of product ideas are no longer adequate to visualize the emerging design spaces where we are facing challenges of large-scale social issues.

A SHORT HISTORICAL PERSPECTIVE ON PROTOTYPING

The activity of prototyping, from the design perspective, has been about making physical artefacts to represent a 'product' before it is completed. Prototypes can be two- or three-dimensional, at a smaller or full scale, high or low fidelity, handmade or machine-made, and so on. Depending on the stage in the design process, prototypes can be used to:

Experiment/explore ideas
Identify problems
Understand and communicate a form or structure
Overcome the limitations of two-dimensional work
Support the testing and refinement of ideas, concepts and principles
Communicate with others
Sell the idea to the client.

The role that prototypes have played in design has changed over the years. In the 1980s prototypes tended to be look-alike models with rich visual detail. They were most often made near the end of the design development process as a means of communicating to (and often convincing) the client what the final product would (or should) look like. Hand skills and craft were critical in the process. Skilled model builders were often an integral part of the design team as the details were often determined in the making (Simons and Sanders 2010). With the introduction of computer modelling tools in the 1990s, the product could be seen much earlier in the design process. Highly accurate machined parts made from the computer-aided design (CAD) data could be more easily produced. Today it can be hard to distinguish a prototype from a manufactured product and, in fact, they may even be the same thing.

The emergence of interaction design as a field and as an offer has also impacted our thinking about prototyping. Early efforts in this field focused on the development of software-based tools for prototyping that attempted to mimic the real thing. But it was soon established that less realistic representations of screens and interaction sequences were actually more useful early in the design process (Rudd, Stern and Isensee 1996). We learned that people are more likely to respond with constructive feedback to a rough prototype of an interactive sequence than to an interactive sequence that looks final. The value of paper-prototyping and the use of Post-it™ notes as a means to quickly mock up information architecture are now well-known design tools in the interactive domain.

There is now a split in the evolution of prototyping. On the one hand, prototypes are more quickly and easily produced in very realistic forms. The value in these forms of prototyping is that you can share (or sell, as the case may be) the idea much more easily, before there is a commitment to tooling or construction. The concept can be shown to potential purchasers who can more accurately evaluate it when it looks, and possibly acts, real. On the other hand (and at the same time), prototypes are taking shape much earlier and in very rough forms. We see this development in the design of both hardware and software. One positive attribute of the trend towards roughness is that prototyping can occur very early in the design process. In fact, it is taking place now throughout the entire design process, with progressively more realism as the process continues. Rapid and early prototyping enables learning through making. Another positive attribute of roughness is that it invites the participation of a wide range of other stakeholders (who are likely to be nondesigners) into the design process at an early stage of the decision-making process.

NEW FORMS OF PROTOTYPES ARE EMERGING

Note that the use of the word prototype in design has focused on the physical manifestation of an idea—that is the object of design. This is so because the traditional design domains have been organized around the object of the design: product design, visual communication design, interior space design, architecture, and so on. The meaning of the word 'prototype' to designers has developed in this context. However, the common meaning of 'prototype' is that it is the first of its kind—the first or preliminary model of something. With this broader definition in mind, we can imagine prototyping to take place not only in space (i.e. physical manifestations) but also in time (e.g. storytelling and scenarios). It is this expanded meaning of prototyping in space and time that will be used in the rest of this chapter.

As the landscapes of design theory and practice have been changing, new types of prototyping have emerged to support and facilitate new ways of designing. Some of these new forms of prototyping are explorations in ways to embody ideas about experience and include empathy probes (Mattelmäki and Battarbee 2002), primes/sensitizing tools (Sleeswijk Visser, Stappers, van der Lugt and Sanders 2005) and video prototypes (Westerlund 2009).

In speculative design, we see another new category of prototyping that includes critical design objects (Dunne and Raby 2001), cultural probes (Gaver, Dunn and Pacenti 1999) and provotypes (Mogensen 1992). Speculative designs are hypothetical products that are meant to challenge narrow assumptions—preconceptions and givens about the role products play in everyday life. Critical designs, probes and provotypes challenge the status quo and make us think about the future implications of what we design and produce.

A DEFINITION OF PROTOTYPING FOR THE NEW DESIGN SPACES

In traditional design spaces, the focus has been on using prototypes to help us give shape to the future—that is to *help us see* what it could be. It has become apparent that prototyping needs to come in many forms so that all kinds of people can participate in the front end of the design process. In the emerging design spaces, on the other hand, the focus will be on using prototyping to help us, all of us, to *make sense of the future*. In the new design spaces, prototypes will not just be seen as representations of future objects but as tools for collectively exploring, expressing and testing hypotheses about future ways of living in the world. With the expanded definition of prototyping, there is a place for everyone at the table.

As the problems that designers deal with become more complex and pressing, it has become apparent that a new design language that everyone can use is needed. Ideas need to be communicated to and understood by others or they will not be made or enacted upon in the future (Westerlund 2009). Prototyping can be a tool for externalizing the visualization process. The participatory prototyping cycle is a positive step forward in that direction.

THE PARTICIPATORY PROTOTYPING CYCLE

The participatory prototyping cycle (PPC) is a framework for action in design (see Figure 4.2). It emerged during reflection on over thirty years of experience in the practice of design research. The PPC acknowledges the need for prototyping

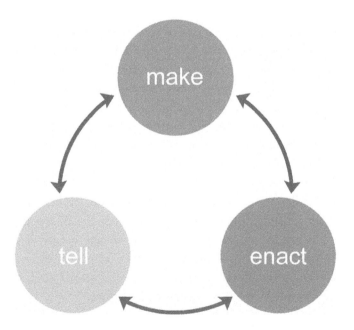

Figure 4.2 Participatory Prototyping Cycle: A Model for Cocreation in Design. The participatory prototyping cycle (PPC) is a framework for action and a model for cocreation in design. Credit: Elizabeth B.-N. Sanders.

Figure 4.3   Participatory Prototyping: Making. An interdisciplinary team is engaged in a collective making experience in the fuzzy front end of the design development process. Credit: Elizabeth B.-N. Sanders.

in space as well as in time. It describes the interplay between making, telling and enacting. Prototyping unfolds as an iterative loop of making, telling and enacting in the future design domains.

In making, we use our hands to embody ideas in the form of physical artefacts. The nature of the artefact changes from early to later stages in the design process (see Figure 4.3). Artefacts made early in the process are likely to describe experiences, while artefacts made later in the process are more likely to resemble the objects and/or spaces.

Telling is a verbal description about future scenarios of use. We might tell a story about the future or describe a future artefact (see Figure 4.4). But this can be difficult for people who do not have verbal access to their own tacit knowledge.

Enacting or pretending refers to the use of the body in the environment to express ideas about future experience (see Figure 4.5). Acting and performance can also be considered forms of enactment that are particularly useful later in the design process. There has been some interest in various forms of enactment as design tools (e.g. Buchenau and Suri 2000; Burns, Dishman, Johnson and Verplank 1995; Buxton 2007; Diaz, Reunanen and Salmi 2009; Oulasvirta,

Figure 4.4   Participatory Prototyping: Telling. This participant is telling future stories about the magical device that she has created that will help her live a better life and manage her Type 2 diabetes every day. Credit: Elizabeth B.-N. Sanders.

Kurvinen and Kankainen 2003; Simsarian 2003), and some of this work has been done collaboratively with end users and other stakeholders.

The PPC is a model for cocreation in design. It invites relevant stakeholders into the design process and supplies them with tools, methods and activities that they can use without having education or experience as designers. For example, making is a skill that many adults do not necessarily feel adequate in using these days. They find it easier to rely on or hire the 'makers' to embody their ideas. Telling and enacting, on the other hand, are skills that everyone has familiarity with and may be more comfortable using, especially in inviting environments. The PPC combines making, telling and enacting and uses each activity to fuel the next. By putting making together with telling and enacting, you can empower people who are not skilled in making to externalize their visualization process.

The differentiating characteristic of the PPC model (versus the other new forms of prototyping) is its emphasis on the cyclical and iterative relationship between making, telling and enacting. You can enter the PPC at any point—that is by *making* things or *telling* stories about the future or *enacting* future experiences. And from each entry point, you can move in any direction as these examples indicate:

> First make a prop and then use it in telling stories about how it might fit into people's future ways of living.

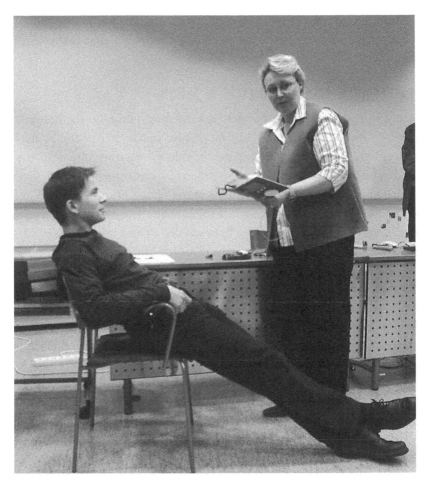

Figure 4.5   Participatory Prototyping: Enacting. A designer and a medical professional enact a situation about the future in which hypothetical mobile technology will enhance the relationship and communication between the patient and the caregiver. Credit: Elizabeth B.-N. Sanders.

Make a prop and enact a scenario of use with it.

First tell a story about the future and then make things that will help you to tell the story more effectively.

Tell or write a story about the future and then enact it using the actual environment as the stage.

First enact a scenario about the future and then make props to help make the enactment more real.

Enact a future scenario and then turn it into a story.

You may find yourself going around several times. For example, you may write or tell a story about the future and then enact it. Then you could make stuff that people would need to live in the story, and enact it again. You may then find that you need to go back and rewrite the story. You might even find that you need to write a new story.

THE PARTICIPATORY PROTOTYPING CYCLE IN ACTION

The squiggle diagram (Figure 4.6) presents the three phases in the design development process today. The large and messy area on the left of the figure is the fuzzy front end where the activities are focused on figuring out what the idea might be. The black dot is the idea. Once the idea has been established, the traditional design process, shown on the right of the figure, unfolds forward in time, becoming progressively more linear and predictable. The overlapping area in the middle around the idea is the bridge between design and research.

How does the PPC work in the design development process? Think of the PPC as a generative seed moving and tumbling across all phases of the design process over time. The leading activity (i.e. making, telling or enacting) will vary by phase. The leading activity may also vary based upon team composition and on the project type.

In general, enacting is the PPC mode that is in the lead in the pre-idea space as shown in Figure 4.7. The purpose of the pre-idea phase is to explore experience (i.e. past, present and future experience) and to understand experience. Enacting is the ideal medium for this. Enacting can be done alone, but the results are far more evocative and provocative when done collaboratively. Enacting will be further synergized when followed by making and telling activities.

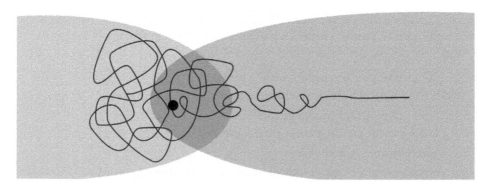

Figure 4.6 The Participatory Prototyping Design Development Process. The squiggle diagram is a three-phase model of the design development process today. The pre-idea space is shown on the left, the cross-over space is shown in the overlap and the traditional design process is shown on the right. The black dot is the idea. Credit: Elizabeth B.-N. Sanders.

Figure 4.7 The Participatory Prototyping Design Development Process: Pre-idea. In the pre-idea space, enactment is the lead activity because the focus is on exploring and understanding experience. Credit: Elizabeth B.-N. Sanders.

Figure 4.8 The Participatory Prototyping Design Development Process: Making. In the cross-over area between research and design, making is the lead activity because visualization of the idea is the key. Credit: Elizabeth B.-N. Sanders.

Making is the PPC mode that is in the lead *on the bridge*—that is, in the cross-over domain between the pre-idea space and the design development process as shown in Figure 4.8. The purpose here is to explore and visualize ideas in order to figure out what the future situations of use might be. The various forms of making give shape to the future. In the bridging stage, making is the focus of the effort, with enacting and telling acting as ways to enrich, extend and extrapolate the made artefacts. The earliest forms of making include maps, timelines and collages. Later forms of making include props, Velcro models and really rough prototypes. The traditional forms of prototyping will be seen later in the design development process.

Telling is the PPC mode that is in the lead later in the design process as shown in Figure 4.9. The purpose of telling is to keep the idea alive and evolving. If a participatory process has been used throughout the process, the primary activities here will be telling or sharing, since buy-in to the idea by the stakeholders is already likely to have occurred. On the other hand, if a participatory process has

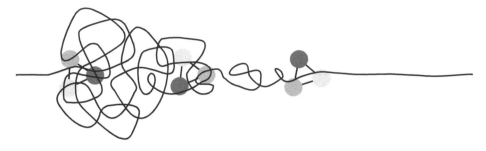

Figure 4.9   The Participatory Prototyping Design Development Process: Telling. In the traditional portion of the design development process, telling is the lead activity since attention must be given to keeping the team on board. Credit: Elizabeth B.-N. Sanders.

not been used, the primary activity can be better described as selling, since the stakeholders who will be affected by the design may still need to be convinced that the idea is good. The earliest forms of telling include descriptions of the made artefacts or the stories that are imagined. Later forms of telling include presentations and selling events.

The primary advantage of the making/telling/enacting model is that it provides for alternative forms of expression for all the stakeholders in the design process. Some people will respond best to stories, some to the enactments and others to the props and models. By utilizing all three in an iterative cycle, everyone who has a stake in the experience domain can contribute to the conceptualization process and find a means of externalizing their visualizations.

THOUGHTS ON THE CURRICULUM FOR DESIGN

The shift from object-oriented designing (where prototyping focuses on physical representations) towards purpose-driven designing (where prototyping takes place in space and in time) will certainly lead to changes in the design curriculum for the future. What does the PPC model imply for design educators?

> We will need to understand what foundational skills are needed for a designer to be proficient in the three modes (making, telling, enacting) and in designing tools for others to use in all three modes.
> We will need to provide even more room for exploration, intervention and experimentation in space and time.
> There will be hands-on courses that focus on provocation and intervention.
> We will teach pretending along with drawing at the start of the design education process.
> We will need to learn from storytellers, performers and sellers.

We will teach telling along with drawing at the start of the design education process.

We will need to further explore all the new forms of prototyping. How rough can they be? How fast can we go?

FINAL THOUGHTS

How will the PPC play out across the design disciplines? For example, will it be different for industrial design versus architecture versus interaction design? Or will the PPC be instrumental in helping to integrate the traditional design disciplines as they are put to use in the emerging design domains that are based on the purpose of the design? Answers to these questions are emerging as the framework has now been used successfully to organize and critically reflect on the very wide ranges of tools and techniques that have been published in the participatory design literature (Brandt, Binder and Sanders 2013).

By repurposing prototyping into a collective activity, our challenge as educators will be to facilitate the relevant and timely application of the PPC. We will need to be clear on what can be learned from each prototyping activity and choose the appropriate methods, tools and materials. For example, how will the properties of the materials involved affect the results of a given PPC activity?

These new views on the scope, nature and purpose for prototyping may help us to realize what it means to bridge the gap: the gap between research and design or the gap between the researcher and the designer. Collective prototyping of activities and artefacts can be the bridge over the gap. They can be what we will walk on to get from the pre-idea space to the end of design development process.

FURTHER READING

Brandt, E., Binder, T., and Sanders, E.B.-N. (2013), 'Tools and Techniques: Ways to Engage Telling, Making and Enacting', in J. Simonson and T. Robertson (eds), *Routledge International Handbook of Participatory Design*, New York: Routledge.

Buchenau, M., and Suri, J. F. (2000), 'Experience Prototyping,' in *Symposium on Designing Interactive Systems, Proceedings of the Conference on Designing Interactive Systems: Processes, Practices, Methods, and Techniques*, New York: ACM Press, 424–33.

Burns, C., Dishman, E., Johnson, B., and Verplank, B. (1995), ' "Informance": Min(d)-ing Future Contexts for Scenario-based Interaction Design', presented at the monthly program of the San Francisco Bay Area chapter of ACM SIGCHI, Palo Alto, 8 August.

Buxton, B. (2007), *Sketching User Experiences: Getting the Design Right and the Right Design*, San Francisco: Morgan Kaufmann.

Cottam, H. (2010), 'Participatory Systems: Moving Beyond 20th Century Institutions', *Harvard International Review*, 31/4, http://hir.harvard.edu/big-ideas/participatory-systems, accessed 15 May 2012.

Diaz, L., Reunanen, M., and Salmi, A. (2009), 'Role Playing and Collaborative Scenario Design Development', International Conference on Engineering Design, ICED '09, Stanford University, 24–27 August.

Dunne, A., and Raby, F. (2001), *Design Noir: The Secret Life of Electronic Objects*, Boston: Birkhäuser.

Gaver, B., Dunn, T., and Pacenti, E. (1999), 'Cultural Probes', *Interactions*, 6/1: 21–9.

Gedenryd, H. (1998), 'How Designers Work: Making Sense of Authentic Cognitive Activity', PhD thesis, Lund University, Sweden.

Graell-Colas, M. (2009), 'Exploring Visual Means for Communication and Collaboration', MA thesis, The Department of Design, The Ohio State University, Columbus.

Halse, J., Brandt, E., Clark, B., and Binder, T. (2010), *Rehearsing the Future*, Copenhagen: The Danish Design School Press.

Heape, C.R.A. (2007), 'The Design Space: The Design Process as the Construction, Exploration and Expansion of a Conceptual Space', PhD thesis, Mads Clausen Institute for Product Innovation, University of Southern Denmark, Sonderborg, Denmark.

Illich, I. (1973), *Tools for Conviviality*, New York: Harper & Row.

Martin, R. (2009), *The Design of Business: Why Design Thinking Is the Next Competitive Advantage*, Boston: Harvard Business School.

Mattelmäki, T. (2006), 'Design Probes', DA dissertation, University of Art and Design Helsinki.

Mattelmäki, T., and Battarbee, K. (2002), 'Empathy Probes', in T. Binder, J. Gregory, and I. Wagner (eds), *Proceedings of the Participatory Design Conference 2002*, Palo Alto: CPSR, 266–71.

Mintzberg, H., and Westley, F. (2001), 'Decision Making: It's Not What You Think', *MIT Sloan Management Review*, 42/3: 89–93.

Mogensen, P. (1992), 'Towards a Provotyping Approach in Systems Development', *Scandinavian Journal of Information Systems*, 3: 31–53.

Oulasvirta, A., Kurvinen, E., and Kankainen, T. (2003), 'Understanding Contexts by Being There: Case Studies in Bodystorming', *Personal and Ubiquitous Computing*, 7/2: 125–34, London: Springer, Verlag.

Rudd, J., Stern, K., and Isensee, S. (1996), 'Low vs. High-fidelity Prototyping Debate', *Interactions*, 3/1: 76–85.

Sanders, L., and Simons, G. (2009), 'A Social Vision for Value Co-creation in Design', *Open Source Business Resource*, December, http://www.osbr.ca/ojs/index.php/osbr/article/view/1012/973, accessed 11 November 2010.

Simons, G., and Sanders, E. (2010), *Thinking about Prototyping*, working paper.

Simsarian, K.T. (2003), 'Take it to the Next Stage: The Roles of Role Playing in the Design Process', presented at *CHI 2003: New Horizons*, Fort Lauderdale, FL, 5–10 April.

Sleeswijk Visser, F., Stappers, P.J., van der Lugt, R., and Sanders, E.B.-N. (2005), 'Context—Mapping: Experiences from Practice', *CoDesign*, 1/2: 119–49.

Westerlund, B. (2009), 'Design Space Exploration: Co-operative Creation of Proposals for Desired Interactions with Future Artefacts', PhD thesis, Human-Computer Interaction, KTH, Stockholm.

ACKNOWLEDGEMENTS

The ideas in this paper have benefited from lively discussions and thoughtful feedback from Carolina Gill, associate professor in design, and from conversations with the first-year graduate students in design at The Ohio State University in 2010.

5 HANDLE WITH CARE

HAZEL WHITE

> 'This is my great grandson playing in Central Park, yesterday—they've all gone to New York for the wedding.' She placed the colourful knitted pincushion in the box and flicked through another set of images.
>
> 'That's your granddaughter isn't it?' said her carer, as she placed a cup of tea next to the intricately inlaid box.
>
> 'Yes, she said she'd put the wedding photos in the box for me on Saturday.'
>
> 'Have all the family gone to the wedding?'
>
> 'No,' she said, placing a soft blue and white pincushion in the box, 'my nephew's family couldn't—what with the new baby, look here he is,' she said as pictures of a sleeping baby appeared on the screen, 'these appeared in the box, the day he was born.'

Imagine that your elderly relatives could view online photostreams using 'knitted remotes' without knowing how to use the internet or even knowing that online photo-sharing exists. The *Hamefarer's Kist* (Figure 5.1) is a suggestion of how older people in care homes could share experiences with geographically distant relatives.

This chapter explores how a craft approach, thinking through meaning and materials, can be used to create artefacts which ask questions about how we might use technology in the near future. The object and interaction being discussed is not a prototype in the traditional product development sense—steps on the way to the manufacturing of a final product—but a speculative object, which engages people in conversations about how technology might be usefully integrated into their lives.

Anthony Dunne (2005) suggests that the craft object and the thinking embodied within it should be considered as genotypes rather than prototypes—that is, as models which contain the 'gene' of an idea, where the value of the object is its content rather than its appearance and technical function. Another difference between the genotype and prototype is that the former is not part of an iterative process between stakeholders in order to identify appropriate technology and engineering requirements prior to manufacturing, for example. Genotypes are embodiments of an idea themselves.

Figure 5.1 *Hamefarer's Kist*, Hazel White with Paul MacKinnon, 2010. Source: Hazel White.

In his essay 'Design Fiction', Julian Bleecker (2009) extends the idea of the genotype by describing 'design fictions' as prototypes of other worlds and other experiences. He describes objects brought back from the future to be studied and meaning ascribed to them: a sort of future archaeology. I have reappropriated Bleecker's Design Fiction as *Craft Fiction* to contextualize and describe *Hamefarer's Kist*, a project where material and technology are given future meaning and purpose through collaborations between hackers and mashers, knitters and photographers, people and stories, creating a networked interactive device to enable older people, health and care professionals reimagine products and services for older people.

The idea for simple interactions has been created by a hybrid craft and design process; material and technical process explorations, mock-ups, test pieces, lash-ups and genotypes are created which allow interaction with a physically embodied idea. This process has produced speculative objects that suggest how we might use the material world to access the digital world. This is an interesting space to explore ideas as it marks a fundamental shift from the studio craft environment—the space where craft makers work, often in solitary practice, giving meaning to material through time, hand skills and long-learned processes—to a space where ideas are tried and tested among potential users and care professionals, including their thoughts and insights in the development process.

Genotypes and design fictions open up an interesting space for the craftsperson to work, suggesting new functions for craft objects in the mediation and understanding of technology—objects which are not simply ways of 'dressing technology', such as jewel-encrusted USB storage devices or novel ways of wearing iPods to the gym, but a way of exploring the multilayered meaning of personal artefacts. For the craftsperson, who is often used to being in command of all aspects of the making process, the idea of a genotype is appealing. Instead of becoming bogged down in technology, which will inevitably become cheaper, faster and smaller, the aesthetics and meaning of the interactions can be explored using low-tech software and hardware, which, if not made by the craftsperson themselves, are created by collaborators who can share in the craftsperson's vision. In the next section, the notion of craft fiction or props for imagining a not-too-distant future is explored from my experience as a trained jeweller and design educator.

HAMEFARER'S KIST

As a lens through which to view the world, jewellery encompasses sociocultural aspects of status, identity and ritual through an exploration of materials, technical processes and hand skills to explore interactions between people, objects and wearability. The New Jewellery Movement of contemporary jewellery, which originated in the Netherlands in the 1960s demonstrated that jewellery could also become sociopolitical, eschewing precious materials and delicate forms in favour of conceptual jewellery that questioned how, where, by whom and why the jewellery pieces were worn. This conceptual approach resonated with and inspired me to develop fictions around jewellery-like objects (e.g. Body Interventions and Telling Tales), as seen in Figures 5.2 and 5.3. This knowledge and experience establishes the basis from which *Hamefarer's Kist* was undertaken.[1]

Hamefarer's Kist explores how older people in Shetland, the islands halfway between Scotland and Norway, might keep up to date with their children and grandchildren using evocative knitted objects to access the internet. In essence, the task performed is very simple; by placing a knitted pincushion in the box, users can select a specific online photostream, which relatives update remotely. More details explaining how this works will be outlined later. The kist was developed whilst I was working as a commissioned practitioner on the major

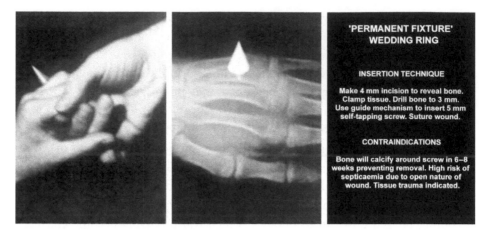

Figure 5.2   Body Interventions: 'Permanent Fixture' wedding ring, Hazel White, 1993.
Source: Hazel White.

Figure 5.3   Telling Tales, Hazel White, 2008. Source: Hazel White.

Arts and Humanities Research Council funded project 'Past, Present and Future Craft Practice' at the University of Dundee and through an artist's residency with Shetland Arts. The project involved a partnership between a variety of people—designers, software developers, knitters and a group of elderly people living in Shetland, who all brought different knowledge, experience and stories to the kist (Figure 5.4).

The original idea was to develop a very personal crafted digital artefact that was evocative of Shetland. My mother's family is from Shetland, and I lived there until I was three years old but had never returned. I proposed to explore how a digital crafted object could create a sense of a Shetland home for Shetlanders living elsewhere, based around gathering family tales. When I arrived in Shetland for a month's residency in August 2009, I quickly realized I was trying to create some sort of nostalgic myth, which, frankly, was not very interesting to anyone besides me. However, in exploring the role crafted objects and stories have for Shetlanders, I began developing an idea of how a digital crafted object might enable Shetlanders to connect to their dispersed families. Shetland is a particular place, outward-looking with a culture quite different from the Scottish mainland. Similar to most of the Highlands and Islands of Scotland, it saw a steady migration of its people in the nineteenth and twentieth centuries to Canada, Australia, New Zealand and to the Scottish mainland—a trend which continues as young people leave the islands to study and seek work, sometimes to return, often not. Since the 1960s Shetland has organized 'Hamefarins', where the diaspora are invited back to take part in festivities and remember their Shetland connections. The traditions of fiddling, Fair Isle knitting and fire festivals are at the forefront. During Up Helly Aa, the best-known fire festival, men dress up as Vikings and burn a painstakingly crafted Viking galley (Figure 5.5). It speaks of a Viking past, but it actually began in the late nineteenth century as a way of pulling the eroding community together. Fiddling is a way of sharing music, stories and cultural identity with former trading partners from the Faroe Islands to Ireland. Knitting was for many an economic imperative, both to make their own clothes from the local wool and to trade. The view of Shetland through knitting, fiddling and fire festivals is what Joseph Church describes as, 'A Tendentious Revision of the Past in the Construction of Community' (1990: 7). But that is what humans do: we create myths and rituals to create a sense of belonging; crafted objects, whether they are Viking Galleys or prayer beads, are part of that sense of belonging.

In keeping with the stereotypes, I spent my first week on Shetland learning to knit the traditional Fair Isle patterns. This enabled me to connect with older people, asking questions in a relaxed way. I heard stories of children and

Figure 5.4 Maggie Leask in her living room, Harlsdale, Whalsay, Shetland, 2010.
Source: Hazel White.

grandchildren who were making lives in mainland Scotland or further afield. I learned that Fair Isle knitting patterns are a form of code: Shetlanders can recognize who knitted them and when, so accurately that they could be used to identify the bodies of fishermen lost at sea. I also learned that the Shetland Community is a collection of shared stories, and every community in Shetland has either a museum or heritage centre. These are where stories are archived, and they contain the often-handcrafted objects around which people tell their stories. I visited a heritage centre on the island of Whalsay, where residents of the local care home were visiting on a day trip. A man who had had a stroke was being shown pictures from an album of wedding photographs. He could not talk, but he could indicate when he recognized someone in the photographs. His carers could fill in the details and tell the story of the people in the photographs; Whalsay has a population of 1,000 people, so stories are communal. Later, while I was visiting a care home, a slideshow of the residents enjoying various day trips was playing on a large flat screen TV. The residents ignored it as it played on a constant loop, and they could not select or stop the images. I began to see how a

Figure 5.5   Up Helly Aa Festival, 2010. Source: Chloe Garrick.

crafted digital object might be a tool for sharing and telling stories. The idea was a sort of knitted iPad—using knitting as the controllers to access online photos. I thought of using the Fair Isle patterns themselves as code, to be optically read; however, to get a plausible working prototype together in the time frame, we used Radio Frequency Identification (RFID) tags (similar to the technology used in toll road prepaid cards).

In developing the idea, I worked with software developer Paul MacKinnon, who developed an iPhone app called Knitted Remote. When a knitted pincushion is placed in the box (Figure 5.6), an RFID reader identifies the online photostream associated with that pincushion, and the app tells the iPhone to display it. The viewer can then flick through the images onscreen or select another pincushion and display a different set of photographs. Each pincushion is associated with a different person, place or event. The photostreams are created online by the technologically savvy younger relatives, in Edinburgh, Sydney or wherever. More photos can be added at any time—they will immediately appear in their relative's kist, in Shetland. The pincushions, knitted by a range of family and friends, have a variety of different colours and textures, making them immediately distinguishable. We used existing technology so that the kist works and is a plausible embodiment of an idea. It has limitations in terms of screen size and

Figure 5.6   An example of a Fair Isle pincushion, knitted by Betty Leask, 2010.
Source: Hazel White.

how the computing is accommodated; however, it is an object with which people understand and engage. It is purposed to do only one particular task, but clearly the kist could be developed in a number of different ways. It has been interesting to use the multifunctional platform of an iPhone to do only one simple thing. There is a need to design for people and place; this is where a craft way of thinking comes into its own. Much technology is arguably developed with either a sleek modernist office or home environment in mind.

Many of our homes in the UK are filled with mass-produced, identikit furnishings and objects rather than individual objects with personal stories. Often older people's homes and rooms in care homes are filled with the personal crafted artefacts that have been acquired over time and have resonance with particular people and events. If we make things for particular people and places, they may have a resonance and meaning for others.

CLOSING COMMENT

The kist was exhibited in the Bonhoga Gallery in Shetland, June 2010, in an exhibition called 'Crossing Points', along with work by Tomoko Hayashi and Stefan Agamanolis of Distance Lab[2] and Dr Sarah Kettley.[3] The exhibition was a means of exploring the embodied idea in a gallery environment. It was presented in the gallery space in the context of a domestic interior with the exhibits displayed as part of the furniture. The kist sat on a sideboard, as it might in the owner's home. The intention was to encourage visitors to interact with it. In observing visitors to the exhibition, it was clear that kindergarten-age children immediately figured out how to use the kist, and that once older users understood how simple it was to use, they too began to feel comfortable with it. Overall, visitors to the exhibition liked the idea of using familiar, tactile objects as controllers and seemed to quickly associate each pincushion with each online album. They could see how they might use the kist and appeared to see the minimal functionality as strength, as evidenced in their comments via the online visitors' book (via Twitter). Visitors wanted to know whether they could purchase the kist for elderly relatives, suggested alternative applications in care homes and schools and commented on how it allowed them to use technology in a painless way.

The development of the *Hamefarer's Kist* has led to a project exploring ways of using technology to share children's stories with the Children's Hospice Association Scotland (CHAS) and enabled a range of medical and care professionals begin to imagine innovative ways of how technology might be humanized.

But what is the significance of the craftsperson's approach? I believe a craft maker pulls out particular qualities of a material, whether that is through knitting or a smart phone. The craft writer David Pye (1968) describes working with walnut: walnut wood in its unselected state is nothing special, but by selecting one specific quality of it, the quality that allows its burr to be polished to highest sheen and acquire a patina over time, it becomes the material of craft. Similarly, the pattern, colour and feel of Fair Isle knitting and the ability of an iPhone to access a specific type of online content make them materials to which a craftsperson can give meaning. Craft practitioners are taking the huge mass of technological possibility and taking a small sliver of it to create meaning through evocative objects. These embodied ideas are interpreted differently by different people: the school teacher sees them as an educational tool, the tele-care manager as a way of increasing uptake of remote healthcare services, the child as a magic pillow.

The Hamefarer's Project has been about humanity, using objects and aesthetics which have personal resonance for individuals and adapting technologies to meaningfully fit their lives. In part, what myself and others working in this area are doing is crafting objects in the service of particular communities to articulate desires and needs in cultural, meaningful ways. We are taking the stuff of gadgetry and adapting it to create objects which are meaningful to people who are not normally considered within the development of these technologies.

The craftsperson's approach to prototyping is to make ideas that you can hold in your hand. Handle with care.

NOTES

1. For further reading about the jewellery design projects and visual work of Hazel White, see, for example, http://hazelsnotes.wordpress.com/interactive-craft/, accessed 1 January 2013.
2. See http://web.media.mit.edu/~stefan/hc/projects/mutsugoto/.
3. Dr Kettley is based at Nottingham Trent University, UK; see www.sarahkettleydesign .co.uk.

FURTHER READING

Bleecker, J. (2009), Design Fiction: A Short Essay on Design, Science, Fact and Fiction, Near Future Laboratory, http://nearfuturelaboratory.com/2009/03/17/design-fiction-a-short-essay-on-design-science-fact-and-fiction/, accessed 9 January 2013.

Church, J. (1990), 'Confabulations of Community: The Hamefarins and Political Discourse on Shetland: Tendentious Revisions of the Past in the Construction of Community', *Anthropological Quarterly*, 63/1: 31.

Dunne, A. (2005), *Hertzian Tales: Electronic Products, Aesthetic Experience, and Critical Design*, Cambridge, MA: MIT Press.

Pye, D. (1968), *The Nature and Art of Workmanship*, Cambridge: Cambridge University Press.

ACKNOWLEDGEMENTS

The Arts and Humanities Research Council funded project 'Past, Present and Future Craft Practice' at the University of Dundee, Scotland. Clair Aldington and Hazel Hughson at Shetland Arts. Betty and Maggie Leask and all the contributing knitters.

6 PROTOTYPES AS A CENTRAL VEIN FOR KNOWLEDGE DEVELOPMENT

PIETER JAN STAPPERS

Research and design are often perceived and presented as two different worlds, occupied by different types of people with different aims. At the one extreme, researchers are viewed as individuals who rationally grow knowledge by a series of experimental tests of hypotheses. At the other, designers are seen as creatively putting new products into the world with little eye for generalization.

In practice, the activities of researchers and designers are more similar than this comparison might lead one to expect. Both are actively engaged in a process that proceeds from a question, problem, opportunity or a status quo, and both are directed at creating something that does not yet exist (either knowledge or product) and that fits into the future.

In the past two decades our group (ID StudioLab, TU Delft) has been undertaking design research, and increasingly we have tried to use designerly ways of finding things out within the research process. Prototypes, 'working models doing something', have been a core part of this effort, both in exploring, validating and communicating about the things we studied. In this chapter, I will try to make sense of what we learned about the value of prototypes for doing research.

PROTOTYPES: THINGS WE MAKE TO FIND OUT THINGS

The term prototype has been around for a long time in product design, traditionally with its industrial meaning 'the first run of a production line', but increasingly used to denote objects made for purposes of exploration and testing. At the 'Prototype: Craft in the Future Tense 2010' symposium (University of Dundee, Scotland), several qualities were mentioned by the speakers, among which that prototypes are:

Unfinished, and open for experimentation
A way to experience a future situation
A way to connect abstract theories to experience
A carrier for (interdisciplinary) discussions

> A prop to carry activities and tell stories
> A landmark for reference in the process of a project.

Common to everybody's understanding is that prototypes are things we make, things which allow us to see how something new might be or might not be through the processes of making and testing. Prototypes are as much about failing and changing course as they are about demonstrating and proving. In that sense, they can be seen as research instruments, both for exploring new directions and for validating expectations.

ACADEMIC DESIGN EDUCATION AND RESEARCH

As mentioned above, research and design are two different things—that is why we have two different words. Research is aimed at creating generalized knowledge—insights which can be applied elsewhere. This usually comes at the expense of narrowing focus and abstraction from the complexities (and wholeness) of the phenomenon in the world. Most often, research is aimed at new insights about the present world.

Design, on the other hand, is aimed at creating products in the world and builds on insights about many aspects but often is not concerned with generalizing these insights (or products). Design is aimed at new products functioning in the future (in commercial reality, often this is an immediate future).

The two have been merging in interesting ways, however. In our own school, this can be seen in increasing attention to research skills in design education, a growing research programme and an increasing number (and percentage) of PhD students having a design background.

The first of these can be regarded as a natural consequence of teaching design at a (technical) university, where engineering and research are part of the overall culture. Students have access to research courses in the Bachelor and Master programmes, and most graduation projects contain a substantial research element in the form of analysing a situation of use, selecting and applying scientific theories on the different aspects of the design project (human, technology and business), and evaluating proposed solutions, if possible, through a working prototype.

Design is increasingly addressing interdisciplinary problems, and our school is fortunate to be sufficiently large (approximately 2,000 students and 100 FTE staff) to have in-house experts carrying out research on many of the elements.

Most interesting (in my view) is the development over the past one or two decades, whereby students with design training have started to undertake PhD research. In the 1980s and 1990s most PhD students had had their training in other, established, disciplines (such as physics, engineering or psychology) with their own established research traditions and techniques. This new generation has been trained in design, making them not only keen to undertake research with holistic qualities and to seek out knowledge which is highly relevant for application by design(ers), but also to apply the methods and techniques from design to use in a research project. Making prototypes and using these to do research (i.e. to develop knowledge) is a key part of this.

PROTOTYPES IN RESEARCH

Within research projects, we see prototypes made for operationalization, validation and exploration, and these uses seem to fit in different research approaches. When I started to work in this context, I remember that researchers (from nondesign backgrounds) liked working with design students in research courses not because the latter were so good at setting up and conducting experiments but because they were so good at operationalization—making concrete stimuli for the abstract hypotheses that the researchers had proposed from theory. In some cases, this was seen as taking some of the cumbersome work out of the hands of the researchers; but the design of stimuli and the questions that were raised also helped to bring forward new directions for the research itself. In other cases, the prototypes were constructed early on in order to position the phenomenon we wanted to study into (observable) existence, not so much to answer predetermined questions or to prove a predetermined point but rather to boldly go where no man (or at least not we) had gone before, to create and probe a possible future.

The two research approaches, testing preconceived hypotheses and reflecting on open-ended exploration, both suggest uses for prototypes. In the former, the prototypes are a design step in a classic research cycle in which a hypothesis is translated into a stimulus. The prototype plays a role in testing the hypothesis. Here, the act of designing is a separate one, needed for the execution of the research, but not for changing its course. In the latter approach, the focus lies on the creative process of designing the prototype, and the emphasis lies on the insights that are generated in devising the prototype. Here, the act of designing is what brings about the knowledge and sets the course of the larger study. Both of these are valuable activities research.

The next section describes one exploratory study and the role that prototypes played in generating and communicating knowledge in and between research projects, largely fitting the open-ended reflection approach.

EXPERIENCE

In the project 'Interaction with structured families of products and product concepts' (1999–2005), PhD student Ianus Keller (2005) studied the way in which designers kept informal collections of visual materials. The project built on the *Ideate (ID8)* computer program in which (computer-supported) tools and techniques were developed to help designers during the early phases of design in which the problem is explored and ingredients for solutions are gathered and explored; this phase is rife with uncertainties, ambiguities, opportunities and creativity, especially visual thinking. Aims of the project included gaining insights into how and why designers maintain visual collections and finding ways in which digital media can support these purposes. Moreover, the project was carried out in the new ID-StudioLab, a collaborative design research environment in which staff, PhD and MSc students participated, with the express aim of creating a community for designerly research, which promotes cross-overs between projects and research groups at the school (e.g. Pasman, Stappers, Hekkert and Keyson 2005; van der Helm, Stappers, Keyson and Hekkert 2010).

Initial exploration in the field and study of the literature already revealed that the problem was multifaceted, with relevant domains being fields that studied formal and informal collections (library studies, databases, media), design theory (especially creativity and design processes) and cognitive science (categorizations). Moreover, there seemed to be little cross-referencing between these fields, and the terminology used in the publications did not connect easily. As an antidote, we decided not to choose a theory or field but to attack the phenomenon itself head-on by setting up prototypes for making the image collection and by exploring possible digital and physical interactions in a variety of setups. The phenomenon under study was largely unexplored, which called for a nontraditional approach to the study. A traditional approach would have been a series of separate steps: first studying the way images are collected, then formulating a theory, designing a new approach, implementing and testing a feasible prototype in a laboratory, and then testing in practice. Instead, constructing the theory, exploring technological means and connecting with practice were conducted as three parallel tracks.

Regarding both these questions (overlapping fields concerning content, parallel streams concerning process), a prototype, or rather, a series of prototypes, served to maintain focus in the project and to define and refine the description and operationalization of the phenomenon under study. Figure 6.1 shows the connections; Figure 6.2 shows two of the prototypes. The first prototype, called TRI, was a general purpose playground set up to explore the possible interactions of interactive projected computer images on three spatial scales—small, medium and large. It was unfinished and could be used to try out and get-to-work (i.e. to *prototype*) interactions with images and collections of images, based on a categorization of spatial interactions typical of design activities (Figure 6.3).

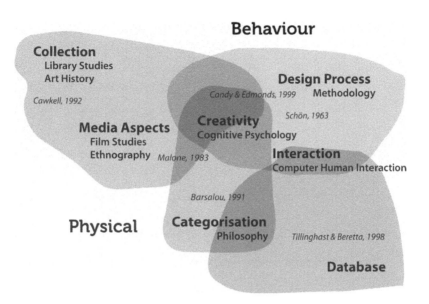

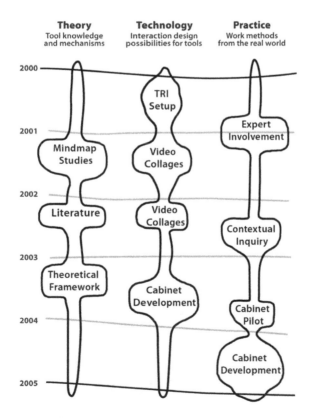

Figure 6.1   Fields (top) relevant for studying image collections of designers, and process (bottom) showed overlapping and connecting elements, which are held together and focused by a series of prototypes. Source: Keller (2005).

Figure 6.2   The TRI (left) and Cabinet (right) prototypes in action. Source: Keller (2005).

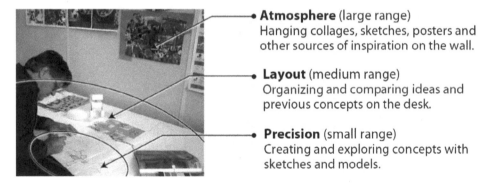

Atmosphere (large range)
Hanging collages, sketches, posters and other sources of inspiration on the wall.

Layout (medium range)
Organizing and comparing ideas and previous concepts on the desk.

Precision (small range)
Creating and exploring concepts with sketches and models.

Figure 6.3   The bodily interactions in design activities can be divided into three spatial ranges, each serving different cognitive functions. Source: Keller (2005: 44).

TRI AND CABINET

The prototype *TRI* can be regarded as an instantiation of the theory in Figure 6.3, and at the same time, it is a means to explore the design solutions afforded by that theory. Its name is a play on the words 'to try' and an acronym for 'Three Ranges of Interaction'. Giving the prototype a clear name helped turn it into a landmark for the project, connecting a theoretical framing to the technical implementation, guiding discussions with visitors and fellow researchers and tying together theory and practice.

The other prototype shown in Figure 6.2, *Cabinet* (again given a distinctive name), was similarly developed in the research studio in close interaction with other PhD students and staff. The Cabinet prototype addressed the question of how designers use their collections of visual imagery that they keep and use for inspiration in designing. Based on a contextual study, Keller (2005) had found that designers keep separate collections of digital and physical images and use them for different purposes. The prototype was developed with two aims: (*a*) to create hitherto nonexisting modes of interaction with images in order to study how users would work with these (see also Keller, Sleeswijk Visser, van der Lugt and Stappers 2009) and (*b*) to instantiate a vision of interacting with two worlds of images in order further the discourse on design, creativity and imagery. Development of a complete and marketable product for storing and sorting images was not a purpose.

During the development of the Cabinet prototype, partial functionalities were tried out by volunteers, who also critically reflected on its merits and deficiencies. And being visible in the studio, both TRI and Cabinet were frequently shown to visiting researchers and discussed with them. These discussions helped to develop the ideas behind the prototypes—maybe even more so than the field testing that occurred afterwards.

HOW THE PROTOTYPES WORKED

In the project, the prototypes served different roles: facilitating discussion, bringing abstract discussions to a concrete level, being visible and reminding other researchers of the project and how they could contribute to or gain from it, posing challenges on how to develop technology to fit the theory or focusing or adjusting the theory towards technologically feasible areas. All together, the prototypes served as a means to promote exploration and reflection as much as (or maybe even more than) means of validation and proof. It helped to ask the right questions (i.e. ones which addressed or connected to the phenomenon of collecting and working with images).

The discussion of, and playing with, the prototypes also played a significant role (though difficult to pinpoint explicitly) in adjacent research projects on design techniques for the early phases in research. Some of the other projects at ID-StudioLab were inspired, informed or otherwise influenced by methods of research, technological effects and discussion of the design decisions that surrounded the prototypes. Examples of these are the PhD projects of Froukje Sleeswijk Visser (2009) and Daniel Saakes (2010). In the former, it informed the methods of deploying prototypes in research—in this case, contextual user studies and interactive communication of the findings. In the latter, it inspired certain visual effects of projecting material patterns over three-dimensional

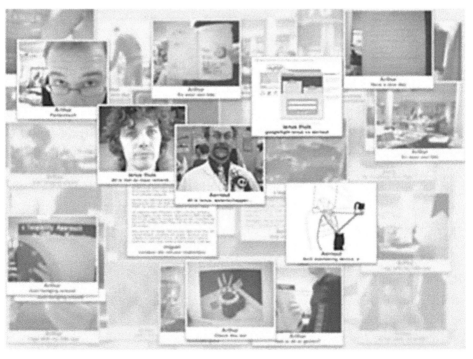

Figure 6.4 Four connected research projects at ID-StudioLab. From top to bottom on this page: projecting material appearance with Skin (Saakes, 2010) and social messaging board (Aernout Peeters). On the next page, from top to bottom, a personal digital sketchbook (Aldo Hoeben), and organizing product images in Productworld (Gert Pasman). Source: Stappers, Saakes, van der Helm and Pasman (2007).

Figure 6.4   (*Continued*)

objects in order to support designers in determining visual appearance of designs. In short, the visibility of the prototypes, the many side-paths that were explored and abandoned, and the discussions they evoked, played a significant part in the neighbouring research. The prototypes allowed reuse of insights in ways not covered by the classical means of research communication, journals and conferences, which typically focus on complete success stories but are not channels to convey the multitude of semisuccessful explorations. Figure 6.4 shows more examples of prototype-based research projects which had such a connection to the TRI/Cabinet research.

This way of working does, however, pose challenges. The technology skills available within the project steer and delimit the scope of the questions. The fanciness of the toy can draw attention away from the topic of study. The prototype can be (and Cabinet certainly has been) mistaken as a product-under-development rather than a tool-to-explore-a-phenomenon (many of the visitors asked when Cabinet would be on the market). And because the discussions and reflections were an ongoing process, it was more difficult to determine areas for publication than if a traditional process with clearly demarcated steps had been followed. Nevertheless, we found that the benefits far outweighed these drawbacks. In focusing the research around the prototypes, and keeping close the theoretical and applied discussions, the work progressed in a way that united theory, technology and practice. The approach yielded a surplus of insights and connections and poses the challenge as to how these insights, which are at very different levels of sophistication and maturity, can or should be gathered, consolidated and shared with the research community.

DISCUSSION: HOW PROTOTYPES WORK IN RESEARCH

How prototypes were used in and around a single research project was outlined in the previous section. From that experience, from the connected research projects and from discussions with others, comes the following tentative list of the designerly functions which prototypes can play in research projects.

1. PROTOTYPES CONFRONT THEORIES

If you are building a prototype that should be used, you cannot hide in abstractions. There is an exigency to translate your theory into the complexity of situations of use rather than conduct an isolated laboratory experiment on an abstracted principle. Typically, building the prototype involves creating a complete solution, which means that multiple theories must be satisfied simultaneously when deciding on the properties the prototype should have. Theories from different areas are required to be brought together and a single phenomenon in the world be used as a carrier that is described from these different perspectives; this in turn helps the creation of links between different fields in interdisciplinary research.

2. CONFRONTING THE WORLD

Whereas the previous principle occurs even before the prototype is working (the confrontations may occur before anything is really made), this principle fits the basics of empirical research: you have got to make it work. Even though your theory might state that something is 'strong', 'fast' or 'thin', making the prototype requires a concrete instantiation: something which is thin is either 1 cm thick or 1 mm thick; something which is fast must arrive within either 1 second or within 1 millisecond. In making such concrete decisions, one can be surprised how many details are just not discussed in the experimental literature.

3. EVOKING DISCUSSION AND REFLECTION

The previous two principles take place whether the researcher works in a studio or works hidden away in isolation. This principle is social and involves other minds. Prototypes have an evocative quality, easily surpassing theories in books or presentations in PowerPoint. They are tangible, hands-on 'things' which speak to the imagination and allow other people (including other researchers) to engage with them and discuss them in the language of everyday experience. In Keller's project, much was learned from the reactions of visiting researchers given a demonstration of the TRI or Cabinet prototypes and from the many suggestions for improvements given by people who played with them.

This evocative social function may be the most important in this list, as it concerns not only generation or validation but also communication of knowledge. In this regard, Mogensen (1992) proposed to speak of provotypes, objects whose function is not to test or prove, but which provoke reflection, experimentation and discussion.

4. CHANGING THE WORLD

This principle is close to action research approaches in the social sciences. The prototype embodies a possible future and allows this to be explored. It can be used as an intervention in a work practice (Cabinet was put into design offices to study how its use of new media techniques affected image collection in practice). In action research methodology, methods have been proposed and developed to document and explain the effects on work practice and thereby better understand this work practice.

5. TESTING A THEORY

This final principle is last in this list not because it is least important, but because it fits in best with the classic experimental approach to research. A prototype can serve as an embodiment for a hypothesis, realizing the conditions (independent variables) in an experiment. It connects to the observation at the beginning of this paper that researchers were so keen on design students because they were great at producing stimuli. This principle fits well into accepted (psychological) research methods, which makes it much easier to publish the research than the previous four.

There is a final candidate which is sometimes mentioned, that prototypes are themselves carriers of knowledge. But although it is clear that prototypes can give powerful illustrations of scientific statements, they do not make a statement in and of themselves. The prototype embodies knowledge only when it is framed within that knowledge. The way and/or context in which the prototype is interpreted must be made explicit for knowledge to be shared and understood. In itself, it is merely a piece of matter, open to interpretation, but incapable of making a statement independent of the interpreter.

CONCLUSION

This chapter has discussed some of the ways in which prototypes, 'things we make to find out things', can play a part in research, 'the bringing about and sharing of new knowledge'. It illustrated some experiences with prototypes in research projects and distilled these down to five principles.

So what is new about this discussion? That depends on the contributor's standpoint. Those who see a great chasm between research (knowledge generation) and design (product development) may not be convinced that the prototype is any more than a convenient implementation of a stimulus. But in this lies a risk of reductionism. As with the students producing stimuli, the step from hypothesis to prototype can be seen as a step that is outsourced by a researcher to a designer.

The history of science and engineering is littered with prototypes. For example, the Wright brothers made the first successful prototype of an aeroplane, and in doing so, they devised a surprising amount of methods, theories and principles. But somehow they became famous for the engineering achievement, not for these related insights. In science, researchers who united fundamental and applied interests achieved great breakthroughs in knowledge development (e.g. Newton, Huygens and Pasteur). Their prototypes likewise enabled and explored phenomena, provided ways to measure, demonstrate, discuss and reflect on them, and validate insights and propositions.

With the growing interest in design thinking, designerly ways of research and for research through design, we can expect a growing understanding of how prototypes are used and how they can play roles in exploring the new, both in research and design.

FURTHER READING

Keller, A. I. (2005), 'For Inspiration Only', PhD thesis, TU Delft, the Netherlands.

Keller, A. I., Sleeswijk Visser, F., van der Lugt, R., and Stappers, P. J (2009), 'Collecting with Cabinet: Or How Designers Collect Visual Material, Researched Through an Experiential Prototype', *Design Studies*, 30/1: 69–86.

Mogensen, P. (1992), 'Towards a Provotyping Approach in Systems Development', *Scandinavian Journal of Information Systems*, 4: 31–53.

Pasman, G., Stappers, P. J., Hekkert, P.P.M., and Keyson, D. (2005), 'The ID-StudioLab 2000–2005', In H. Achten, K. Dorst, P. J. Stappers and B. de Vries, B. (eds), *Design Research in the Netherlands 2005*, Eindhoven, the Netherlands: Eindhoven University of Technology, 193–204.

Saakes, D. P. (2010), 'Shape Does Matter', PhD thesis, TU Delft, the Netherlands.

Sleeswijk Visser, F. (2009), 'Bringing the Everyday Life of People into Design', PhD thesis, TU Delft, the Netherlands.

Stappers, P. J., Saakes, D., van der Helm, A., and Pasman, G. (2007), 'New Media Tools to Support Design Conceptualization', in L. Rothkrantz and C. van der Mast (eds), *Euromedia 2007. Thirteenth Annual Scientific Conference on Web Technology, New Media, Communications and Telematics Theory, Methods, Tools, and Applications*, Ostend, Belgium: EUROSIS, 5–10.

Stappers, P. J. (2005), 'Creative Connections: User, Designer, Context, and Tools', *Personal and Ubiquitous Computing*, 10/2–3: 95–100.

van der Helm, A., Stappers, P. J., Keyson, D., and Hekkert, P. (2010), 'The ID-StudioLab 2005–2010: Further Developing a Creative Research Environment', in H. Achten, B. de Vries and P. J. Stappers (eds), *Design Research in the Netherlands 2010*, Eindhoven, the Netherlands: Eindhoven University of Technology, 65–78.

7 TECHNE AND LOGOS AT THE EDGE OF SPACE

CONSTANCE ADAMS

INTRODUCTION: FUTURECRAFT

With one footstep inside the twenty-first century, humanity is advancing at a rate beyond our entire species' experience. Half a century ago, we had just developed the jet aircraft engine and learned that there was no barrier preventing us from exceeding the speed of sound; we had standardized analogue signals technology for communication across much of the globe and were conducting our first experiments with orbital engineering. All of this took place in a tense and polarized world more heavily armed than ever before. Any developed-world kid with access to information and common resources could build a telephone, a radio or record player, or learn to fix the family's car and household appliances. Any developing-world kid could make a fire, pluck a chicken and build a common tool and might expect to learn more skills as Western culture spread. Both kids knew where their clothes were made and generally where the food had come from that they ate for dinner at night.

Today, fifteen nations are sharing the use of a jointly built permanent platform in space, collaborating despite great cultural and political differences. Not all of the member nations are formally at peace with one another; not all are counted among the developed world. Images of our planet from afar, captured forty years ago, have radically changed the tribal sense of loyalties and territory that helped *Homo sapiens* survive the ice age. Replacing the tribe-nation in this part of the world is a much larger identity structure that places the individual's knowledge-group within a planetary context, blotting and eventually erasing millennia-old boundaries between peoples, nations and ideologies. Awareness of systemic patterns of weather around the globe has begun to bring us solutions to local problems, even as the same global view has shown us the danger of climate change and the role played by local interventions. In the human spaceflight programme, the most technologically advanced countries are learning to collaborate and are dedicating resources to the advancement of knowledge of our planet, our universe and ourselves. Together, we hold within our grasp the capacity to send people to Mars.

And yet a gap is growing between those equipped with the basic skills of life and those without. This gap is an inversion of the standard-of-living gap or the life-expectancy gap, both of which detail the staggeringly greater fortune of our developed-world kid over her sister in the developing world. The former is said to have every possible advantage over the latter and is estimated to use between twenty-five and forty times as many natural resources from birth to adulthood. She is healthy, secure and profligate; and without knowing or intending it, she is threatening the balance of the biosphere. She is unlikely to have any idea about the origins of the things she consumes, where they come from and how they are made. She could no more build an MP3 player than spin, dye and weave herself a coat; and she would be more likely to fly a plane than learn either of these skills.

What we are confronting amongst the most powerful on our planet is a critical dissonance between *techne*—tools, or skill—and *logos*—knowledge, understanding. On the one hand, it is in our collective interest to continue the current rate of increase in learning and applied science in order to beat the rate of climate change and fulfil what may be the biologically programmed destiny of our species; on the other, we are running the risk of stumbling into a profound ignorance in body-based knowledge—that is, the understanding of balance, form and purpose that is learned by working with one's hands.

In this essay on the future of craft, I intend to reconsider the human relationship with tools and form-making in terms of *Homo sapiens astronauticus*. From our perspective at the edge of space, humanity has played a strikingly unique role in the earth's biological history, and craft lies at the heart of it. While the way forward seems clear for the technologies of rapid prototyping and manufacture on which space architects and mission planners expect to rely, it is not clear that this direction is wholly positive. What capabilities are needed and wanted for the missions we must undertake in the foreseeable future? Have we evolved sufficiently in the past two generations to move beyond the relationship between body and thought that has characterized the making of things since the beginning of our time? Here in the doorway to the solar system, how shall we make the things we need and resolve our species-history with the future? I believe that the answer will be multidimensional, technical and physical; it cannot be one or the other.

FRANKENSTEIN'S MONSTER

Mary Shelley modernized the ancient tale of the person who 'knows too much' in her novel *Frankenstein*. By painting a tender and sympathetic picture of the brilliant doctor and the altruism that leads his medical research, she brings the reader along in curious assent with his experiment to emulate the creation of life from pure physical properties. These sympathies reach their conflicted peak in the monster himself: no mindless Golem of the moralizing past, but instead a disfigured child, miserable in his failure to attract affection from a world he needs but does not understand. Painting the monster and his creator with a compassionate brush, Shelley replaced the taboo that previously attached to true innovators (sorcerers, witches, heretics) with a sense of moral complexity that characterizes much of the industrial age.

Anyone raising a small child will attest that the onset of mobility between twelve and eighteen months brings with it a sudden resistance to strange or new foods. The logic of this coincidence is clear from the perspective of evolutionary biology: as long as it is attached to its mother, the child can trust whatever food it is given; but once it can wander off on its own into the fields nearby, this trust must be abandoned. Once they can walk, only the children who fear and refrain from eating unfamiliar things are likely to live to adulthood.

No doubt a similar reflexive fear followed our hominid ancestors throughout their lives, keeping the tribe alive through adherence to the known in a world governed by forces they could not control and could only understand through limited observation and oral tradition. A natural tension exists between the conservative tendency this fear represents and the progressive tendency of curiosity; and from time to time, groups have seen fit to revise old stories of witchcraft and sorcery in order to resist accepting a radical change to their worldview. Often, the history of science and ideas has been one of innovative thinkers burned at the stake for considering new ideas that threatened the dominant structure of things, only to be revived and lionized a few generations later as the insightfulness of their observations becomes clear and the social fabric sufficiently prepared to accept the philosophical challenges they represent.

But the child matures into a person who can balance caution with curiosity. He learns to think for himself.

It is not pandering to our time to find hope in the comparative dominance of ambiguity and complexity in our morality tales. Today, in the developed world, there seems to be a general understanding that new scientific ideas or medical procedures may bring discomfort; that new particle reactors will cause some critics to cry 'Armageddon' until proven safe; that new things may challenge our moral compass but will not necessarily derail our very existence. Probably this change of atmosphere stems from the sheer frequency and number of world-altering new ideas we encounter every year; where Galileo and Copernicus were outstanding heretics of their generations, today we have verified the rate of expansion of the universe, confirmed the existence of liquid water on Mars, discovered the existence of dark matter and begun the genotyping of Neanderthal Man all within one decade.

For those of us working to design the world of *Homo sapiens astronauticus*, the need to negotiate this kind of ethical idea-shock is a regular phenomenon. Almost all new discoveries hold the potential to wipe out humanity if misused, yet they also offer potential solutions to thorny problems. One always asks oneself, 'If I were looking back on this decision from a century in the future, would this idea look quaint or stupid, or simply obvious?' Only very rarely is there an answer.

MISSION TO MARS

At the turn of the millennium, in response to some prodding from friends, I wrote a Mars mission screenplay. It was a liberating experience because I could develop a mission architecture not for today or for twenty years hence, but for whatever future date would be required to allow the development of the technology we really need to do the job—and this is when I first started thinking about rapid prototyping and manufacture.

I had been working for several years at that point on different components of the NASA Mars 'Design Reference Mission' (DRM), principally designing, outfitting and integrating the long-duration crew vessels for the six-month zero-gravity transit phase between planets[1] and for the fourteen-month planned stay on the surface of Mars.[2] Any component of this mission would have to sustain launch and landing loads of up to 7G, operate for at least three years in variable gravity conditions without requiring repair or replacement, sustain up to 125 kg impact load and weigh as little as possible so as to minimize the cost at a minimum of $100,000 per kilo to the surface of Mars. The population of probable users consists of half a dozen humans of mixed gender and race, in early middle age, each holding multiple advanced degrees and capable of assuming responsibility for at least two primary functions and three more secondary functions during the mission. Spacecraft structures would ideally serve multiple systems architectures simultaneously in order to minimize the support mass for life support, avionics, communications, electrical, thermal and crew systems on board.

As an architect one does not usually pioneer the basic technical concept; one's role is to see an idea developed by some group of engineers and to apply it usefully and elegantly into the overall design. With these criteria in mind—robustness, elegance and the ability to address known issues—the overall mission concept that we were asked to support began to sound less than ideal: launching a series of modules to Mars, landing them in precise formation and robotically assembling them into a surface habitat the crew could use once they arrived. Mars is a planet covered in familiar minerals, with several potential power sources available and some water to boot. Everything necessary to build what we need is already there. The only thing missing is the technology to do so.

AEROCAPTURE

In Hollywood terms, the ability to imagine something is all that is required to make it exist. This is useful and a reality that also mirrors the one at the heart of the storyline for 'Aerocapture', a script about an early human mission to Mars during which the habitat itself becomes a Frankenstein's monster for the new millennium. This comes to pass when the robotic manufacturing equipment carrying the blueprints for the astronauts' facilities is damaged upon braking at the Martian atmosphere, leaving it functional but with an unshielded electric charge within its molecular-level building platform. When this super-advanced construction system meets a colony of extremophile bacteria (Ward 2007; Ward and Brownlee 2003) in the rock strata under the building site, the result is a series of morphological changes in the habitat's design driven by what is essentially alien RNA. When the crew arrives twenty years later, they find facilities that they need, but not what they were expecting, and when it becomes necessary to use the same system to build a new spacecraft for the return to Earth, the old conflict between curiosity and superstition emerges.

The irony is not lost on the crew: the very 'Martian life' that these scientist-astronauts had embarked on this five-year trip to find had instead found them—right where they lived. On the journey back to Earth, the crew must contend with species paranoia in opposition to the scientific fascination of finding the object of their original quest embedded in this new form around them, keeping them alive in interplanetary space.

NEXT GENERATION RAPID-PROTOTYPING AND IN SITU MANUFACTURE

In fact, the technology envisioned in 'Aerocapture' is a fusion of CAD/CAM,[3] rapid prototyping and nanotech manufacturing techniques with an artificial intelligence–driven robotics package. With these capabilities—at least two of which are still only conjectural—designed components are built from the molecular level, permitting a symbiotic integration of systems with primary and secondary structure. For example, chains of copper molecules can be formed along ribs in a structure, with carbon molecules surrounding them, permitting the component to dispense with electrical wiring; or a series of optical crystal chains can be manufactured into the webbing of a wall, allowing for integrated data conduction or transmission of external light into a windowless space. Built this way, the entire structure is essentially prewired for remote sensing of all kinds, a completely 'intelligent' house. And because of the robotic/intelligent driver system, the entire manufacturing package can be deployed remotely to work with little or no supervision, using local materials and supplying its own power.

Similar but considerably less complex (and less capable) are the advanced rapid-prototyping and manufacture systems being attempted by various shops today. Essentially advanced CAD/CAM systems, tomorrow's rapid prototyping, will do away with the seams between design and modelling—or rather, between drafting and modelling—and will be able to use a range of materials such that a successful prototype can be instantly reproduced as an engineering unit ready for use. For a long-duration space mission without regular resupply capability, such a system is really a necessity, preferably preprogrammed with the drawings of all components and subcomponents on board so that any spares can be produced without the need for carrying unnecessary items.

WE ALL NEED SPARES

The International Space Station (ISS) requires thousands of kilos of On-orbit Replacement Units (ORUs) per year to keep its various systems functioning. Some components, which are deemed too labour-intensive or unsafe for the crew to disassemble and repair in flight, are replaced wholesale, while others are more readily tinkered with in an attempt to fix. Although the original plans for the Space Station involved the crew spending most of their days in space-performing scientific experiments, the reality of life on orbit has reprioritized their time with a sizable chunk dedicated to Station logistics, housekeeping and maintenance. In other words, no matter how carefully the hardware is designed, how intensively screened for safety and reliability and how expensively prepared for launch, space components break down at least as often as their household versions on Earth.

The problem is, an astronaut on duty cannot simply walk down the street to the hardware store to find a spare gasket, o-ring or light bulb when one breaks. No matter the type, all cargo costs on average $25,000 to launch from the surface of the earth to the Station in Low Earth Orbit (LEO), about 240 miles above us. For this reason, the Station is small compared with any surface laboratory, and as a result, there is very little room on board for stowing anything but necessities. Excess stowage clogs up the already stingy open volume, reducing the ability of the crew to operate and threatening the general air flow, which must be maintained by constantly operating fans to prevent asphyxiation in the gravity-less environment.

So, replacement parts cost the same no matter when they arrive on board, but if all the spare parts one might need cannot be stowed on board, a launch-on-demand system must be established. This requires the ready availability of a number of spacecraft, rapid turnaround time and sufficient total flights to ensure that there is always room in the cargo hold for emergency items on every flight.

In the late 1980s Seven-Eleven Japan pioneered a groundbreaking low-inventory system that serves as the gold standard for efficiency in low-volume, high-traffic applications. Because real estate in Tokyo is so valuable and expensive, convenience stores had to be designed at a minimum size; but unless each store offers a certain array and variety of goods, it is not really very convenient. So the trade-off was made between transportation costs and real estate, and a system was established that permits each store manager to maintain a full inventory but stock only one or two units of each item at a time. As soon as the cash register reports its sale, a call goes to a warehouse outside of town, which puts replacement goods in a small van for rapid inventory replenishment—often within the hour.

When the Space Shuttle's designers originally began planning the reusable Space Transportation System, the DRM was for some twenty-five flights per year, or two each month—one from Florida and one from Vandenberg Air Base in California.[4] However, the realities associated with safe maintenance and operation of such advanced, risky technologies as human-rated spacecraft have meant that the few Shuttle flights achieved per year were inevitably oversubscribed in terms of manifest both up and down, and the Seven-Eleven model is not possible.

For the time being, the ISS programme must juggle the insistent maintenance demands of a thousand unique, critical systems of various origins with the logistical constraints imposed by a limited launch schedule. This challenge is nothing compared with an expeditionary mission to another planet. Beyond LEO, there is no resupply possible, nor any rapid return; everything you take with you must work, and you must take everything you need. Because a Mars mission is more than two decades out, there is sufficient time to look at various options that may no longer be useful for ISS. One approach would be to push for the development of a portable rapid-manufacture system and then require all other equipment on board the spacecraft to be built; any spares could be made from the same material matrix. Another would be to identify a few basic materials whose properties cover all necessities and to develop separate rapid-manufacture systems capable of working with each. Probably the most reasonable and achievable solution would be a combination of the two: hardware developers would be required to stay within a short list of materials for all uses, and rapid-manufacturing systems could be designed as a suite of machines, each able to make parts from one or another family of materials.

Would it be worth developing such a technology for a unique mission? I believe so. There is no question that other remote locations exist for which a suite of flexible rapid-manufacture systems would be well suited, including in small developing communities where the import of exotic technologies to serve the people's sanitation or medical needs brings with it the threat of costly or impossible repairs when crucial components eventually wear out.[5] The main drawback in this kind of application is cost. Once available, however, it is likely that a suite of rapid-manufacture platforms could be highly prized by small businesses that wish to offer a number of products but cannot afford the overhead involved in having a full run of each made and stored. It could also serve in larger industries to generate the capacity for less costly production of custom products, such as cars, shoes or other vehicles.

Inevitably, it would also be used for more advanced modelling and prototyping, and as such, its impact might be less positive than cost effective.

PROTOTYPE AND PROCESS

Today, rapid prototyping is just sufficiently available to make hands-on prototyping obsolete in terms of time, reliability and reproducibility but not sufficiently available to be less expensive or more responsive as a design tool. The central element driving the move to machine prototyping is the use of electronic models as the primary documents for building and manufacture. In seeking to prepare any object for realization, the contemporary designer/architect must generate a virtual model of it. The advantages of doing so are the purity of the geometry, reproducibility of every form and the fact that no further documentation need be generated for manufacture once a prototype has been accepted. Using these models one can send out orders for building components that would have been considered unique in the past and can reuse the same irregular forms repeatedly without a loss of fidelity.

Disadvantages to construction based on electronic models, however, do remain: the loss of handicraft in the modelling process itself, the loss of aesthetic in the regularity of machined forms and the loss of body-knowledge in the design development process. This last drawback now makes itself felt all too often from the outset of design. When the sketching and modelling that once constituted the idea exploration phase of design has moved into the electronic realm, an enormous part of the designer's total intelligence is lost. When manually prototyping an already conceived design, the maker's hands are in the middle of the process, offering nonverbal feedback based on texture, ergonomics and proportion; a machined prototype, on the other hand, offers no feedback beyond the purely logistical (e.g. does it snap together properly, is this airhole in the right place). In other words, what one loses in handing the prototyping process over to the machine is the value inherent in the process itself.

Design does not take place in an instant. Like the multipartner choreography of a Virginia Reel, the design process intertwines need, desire, context, material, inspiration, history, capability and value.

MÉTIS

Craft, mother of Wisdom:

The Greek pantheon personifies what we call 'craft' or 'skill' in the goddess Métis, the first wife of Zeus. One day, tired of his pregnant wife's ill mood, Zeus challenged her to a game of charades: they would take turns changing form to challenge and amuse one another. At one point in this game, though, Métis turned herself into a fly—and Zeus swallowed her. So it was that Métis spent her confinement inside Zeus's head, and that, in giving birth to a baby girl, she gave him such a terrible headache that Hephaestus was called to split open his brother's skull to relieve the pain. Because she emerged into the world from her father's head, the goddess Athena was also known as *parthenos*, or one 'not-born-of-woman'. She is more generally known as the goddess of wisdom and strategy and as the owner of the protective shield Aegis.

If the myths of the Greek world have an outsized influence on Western culture, it is not for want of insight. The story of Athena Parthenos parses out very cleanly: *métis*, or craft, is the mother of wisdom and strategy.

For centuries it has been true that students and practitioners of architecture tend to carry sketchbooks with them everywhere. Even today, when such baggage might seem too bulky, any paper to hand becomes a sketchbook in an instant. The fact of learning to sketch by hand alongside the mastery of calculus, fire codes and the properties of materials makes the design professions increasingly unusual. Despite the growing pressure toward specialization and branding, we combine practical applied engineering with the study of the laws of perspective and line weight, mastering a range of drawing techniques. Even though architecture schools all over the world today are filled with computer-based drafting platforms, networks and printers, the choreography of the conceptualization process continues to play out through handiwork in a dialogue with electronic modelling. What the computer can teach the draftsperson is whether or not the chosen numbers are symmetrical in an array; it cannot impart learning about grace, clumsiness, commodity or elegance.

In this same way, machine-made objects are merely a faithful reproduction of the information originally input. They cannot teach the designer anything through their making, nor do they offer resistance in some parts and flimsiness elsewhere. The only way to restore a physical intelligence feedback loop into a machine-based prototyping and manufacture process would be to develop an interface for the craftsperson that is haptic, feedback enabled and independent of such recent timesaving input tools as the keyboard and mouse.

One Hollywood technology that might point the way is the three-dimensional feedback mechanism depicted in the movie *Iron Man*: a haptic interface area generated by laser sight mechanisms feeding information back to the computer. In this space, the designer's hands and arms become direct input tools, and each gesture is interpreted in its full spatial presence. Although the movie's protagonist Tony Stark uses this would-be tool primarily for file management, one can imagine its true potential as an ability to track hand movements in actual space by laser-modelling the user's hands, and as a way to convert that series of gestures into a virtual model that can then be reviewed and edited using the same motion-capture interface.

Most importantly, this kind of technology can be adapted for deployment without adaptation to variable gravity environments. Whereas most traditional crafts and the electronic interfaces that are replacing them both require that the operator have a flat surface on which to work and tools that will remain on that surface during deployment, a haptic feedback-enabled motion-capture interface takes place in free space without reference to a local vertical other than that of the operator's own body. In other words, these systems could be used equally well on Earth, in space and even on another planet. This may seem like the ultimate niche market to today's readers; but from the perspective of *Homo sapiens astronauticus*, our space-faring great, great-grandchildren, it may be one of the enabling technologies of the twenty-first century.

Ultimately, there is no substitute for the human hand. In his novel *Cherokee*, Jean Echenoz (1983) describes the awakening of thought throughout the body of the narrator/protagonist, a man who had suffered a traumatic accident and is considered brain dead. The premise of the book is that the brain is not the sole repository of thought or personality. Essential aspects of thinking and being reside throughout the body and have been short-changed by Western medicine's obsessive focus on the brain.

PEGGY, DAN AND LONGBOW

Homo sapiens astronauticus is an idea about our collective future. In this idea, the science our space programmes have carried out in order to identify, characterize and learn about our effect on the earth and its atmosphere is embraced, researched and applied in the form of methods for reversing the pathologies we have introduced to the global systems on which we all rely. Unlike *Homo sapiens sapiens, Homo sapiens astronauticus* understands that human survival depends on the preservation and promotion of our planet's biodiversity, and that collective action supersedes tribal aspirations or individual desires. *Homo sapiens astronauticus* may identify tribally but does not do so competitively.[6] Most importantly, this future human acts in a manner that enables the Gaian biome to expand and flourish, a reversal of the current trends toward contraction and death.

If any people alive today are leading the curve in this social evolution, it must be the astronauts and cosmonauts who support our joint space programme, and the engineers who collaborate to enable their work. Certainly it is true that no matter how refined our technologies, at some point everything breaks and will require repair. Failure to recognize this fact has brought down more than one advanced programme, and heroic repair stories are as rich a tradition in spaceflight as heroic rescues are for the rest of us. One such story unfolded a few days into the two-week mission of STS-120, a Shuttle mission to the ISS, whose primary goals included the delivery, deployment and activation of the last major solar arrays on which the growing outpost would depend to meet its power needs. Two members of the Shuttle crew spent a day performing an extravehicular activity (EVA), decompressing overnight in the airlock before donning spacesuits and venturing outside the Station into space in order to remove the arrays from the Shuttle's payload bay and install them on the external truss that serves as the ISS's spine and main power bus. These astronauts had trained for hundreds of hours to learn the skills they would need to perform their tasks, and they performed them precisely according to plan.

However, as the array unfolded, the crew watching through the Station's external cameras noticed that one side of the thin foil that makes up the array had snagged on the guide wire and begun to tear. When the array's motor was commanded to retract and redeploy, the tear became worse. Without this array, the Station would not have enough power to complete its assembly to its full-planned size, and even if it were to finish deploying successfully, the small torn section could cause electrical arcs that would endanger the Station's external systems and any nearby crew members on future EVA sorties.

Within a few hours, the prime Station crew had pulled out spare materials—wire, special Teflon tape, the basic tool kit—and started experimenting with methods of building card-sized foil sutures that would allow an EVA crew member to complete the deployment of the solar panel by fastening the torn sides of the foil back together without incurring an electric shock. In zero G (i.e. zero gravity), doing such a simple tinkering task can become surprisingly complicated, and this job appeared to require all the cooperation, creativity and craft the crew could muster. Peggy Whitson, the Station commander at the time, and her crew mate Dan Tani, were both known for their incredible productivity while on orbit, and perhaps it was especially fortunate that they were the team on orbit to support this particular mission. Before the next day's scheduled sortie, the crew managed to make many special photovoltaic sutures. And so, the ISS solar array was saved from an early demise by a combination of fortunate crew selection and dedicated work, mixed with a dollop of métis.

Craftiness or handiness with tools is, it turns out, one of the most prized qualifications in Space Station crew members. Although not among the official astronaut office selection criteria, time has shown that astronauts with the usual array of advanced degrees and other qualifications, who also spend their spare time building engines, doing carpentry or just fiddling with things, are more likely to have an overall positive effect on the Station workload. Despite the plans for a marvellous, preactivated science laboratory in space, the crew spends a large share of their time—which some estimates value at around $200,000 per hour if all the support cost is included—tinkering in zero G.

'SCRAPBOOKING' TO SCRIMSHAW

Perhaps the most important question regarding the future of craft is: why has handiwork been so seriously devalued in our society? Evidence abounds everywhere that so-called effort-saving devices universally cost extra effort in tinkering, coaxing and repair and in total do not save as much time or work as anticipated. Yet the ability to fix such tools has fallen further and further down in our estimation, until it is assumed when most things break that one will dispose of them and purchase a new one rather than have it fixed. Part of the reason for this is simple: there is almost no one left in the average developed-world town who fixes broken things.

Among those who can afford to spend spare time on hobbies, it is remarkable how many people take to pastimes that are useless in the developed world but are staples of life elsewhere: knitting, quilting, needlepoint, carving, building motorcycles, painting ceramic figurines. Even the craze for assembling elaborate scrapbooks to commemorate with intricately collaged pages every high point in ordinary lives shows that people who have days of remarkable ease do not necessarily want to give up the creative use of their hands. However many machines we may deploy to save us effort, however many little green lights we may have on around us after we turn in at night, even in our leisure, we need to have something to do.

For a crew to embark on a journey to Mars, the outbound or inbound legs of which will take about six months each way, psychologists have expressed concern that boredom may be a significant problem. If, however, the astronauts are not constantly busy with their fitness and maintenance tasks, it is reasonable to imagine that they will find a form of craft to occupy themselves, much like the sailors on whaling ships once carved scrimshaw in their bunks. Without a supply of whalebone or other windfall material at hand, it is interesting to imagine what these activities might be and what intriguing artefacts of the future they will produce.

CONCLUSION

GAIA'S CHILDREN

James Lovelock's Gaia hypothesis[7]—that the wildly diverse forms of life on this planet constitute a part of a total, complex organism much as our bodies are composed of thousands of bacteria that enable their most basic functions—has its ardent followers and detractors in every field. Whether or not one agrees that this enfolding world-being corrects itself in order to maintain its optimal balance, the concept of the Gaian being is extremely compelling. Certainly, this paradigm is consistent with relationships we see everywhere around us, from our own gastric tract to acres-wide aspen growths or the organic symbiosis that effectively covers the entire ocean floor. Let us imagine for a moment that this might be so: that our planet's living layer is one massive, complex super-organism.

HOW MIGHT ONE TEST SUCH A HYPOTHESIS?

Recent discoveries in earth science, geology, oceanography and astrobiology (also known as 'xenobiology', or the study of life away from the earth) of living things that require almost nothing to live have reduced the possible approaches to testing this idea to a single criterion: does it reproduce? In other words, does Earth's biosphere have a means of spreading itself, of multiplying its existence, of propagating its kind?

Next to this question, I picture the problem of humankind among the intelligent species. Of the several species that may now be considered intelligent and of all the creatures on Earth, we alone make tools. From the perspective of *Homo sapiens astronauticus*, it is clear that nothing happens in nature without a reason. Not one of our supposedly vestigial organs is useless; no activity on Earth or in the cosmos is without purpose. If it appears to be so, this is only because the portion of it we have observed thus far is too puny to have captured the larger meaning involved and because we are too impatient to wait for the full evidence to arrive.

Jumping out in time to an eon-cruising time lapse perspective, imagine the history of life on Earth in a minute or two. Picture our planet, over there, about the size of a basketball. First, the shifting shades of atmosphere; then the oceans, the slow spread of blue and then green. Eventually tiny bits of motion can be detected, and herds of creatures roam in the water and on the land. Fires, and storms; the usual cosmic collisions here and there shake things up; then, just near the end, some cities—some lights visible in the night sky. And finally, a few tiny specks begin to pop up into view, jumping off the planet, making tools, vehicles capable of taking them to an asteroid, to another planet . . . where they settle. They bring basic symbionts with them: plants, fish, small food animals; and when they have a critical mass, they begin terraforming the planet. They literally 'make it like Earth'.

We are just imagining here.

But in this story, the tool-making life form has a purpose, which is not to have dominion over the animals or mastery of any kind. This species is the gamete form of the biome: it is the means by which Gaia reproduces. Its purpose—our purpose—is to ensure that our biome survives by sailing to other worlds, and making them live.

In this story, our tools and our craft are our entire purpose. We are pointless without them.

NOTES

1. The first space inflatable habitat spacecraft, TransHab (short for transit habitat), was developed by a NASA and contractor team at the Johnson Space Center from 1997 to 2001. The author was responsible for Vehicle Architecture and Crew Accommodations.
2. Various surface habitation studies, including the NASA-JSC BIO-Plex project and Lunar-Mars Life Support Test Project, Mars Arctic Research Station and the Surface Endoskeletal Inflatable Module (SEIM). See note 1 above.
3. Computer-aided design and computer-aided manufacture.
4. However, when the administration that succeeded the Kennedy–Johnson years took a pen to the budget, that second design iteration was struck from existence. Instead of revising the advertised capability downward to reflect the new reality, managers continued to press the personnel on the ground for double-digit launches per annum. The highest number of flights ever achieved in one year was eleven—or, more accurately, ten, because the eleventh launch resulted in the loss of the Space Shuttle Challenger and her crew.
5. 'Water for Two Worlds: Designing Terrestrial Applications for Exploration-class Sanitation Systems', 2004, NASA Technical Reports Server, http://en.wikipedia.org/wiki/Constance_Adams, accessed on 6 December 2010.

6. Tribal identification refers to a tendency to identify oneself by ethnic and cultural background (i.e. I am a Hawaiian of Chinese descent; I am a Mongolian Russian, etc.), which people in this context are choosing to do all the more readily now that a basic degree of cultural parity/similarity has been achieved. Within this emerging type, intertribal conflict (Russians versus Americans, Africans versus Europeans, etc.) is pretty much a thing of the past, and there is no longer a need to assimilate at the expense of one's heritage. Probably one factor is the high degree of assimilation already achieved, which may sound cynical, but let's be realistic: cosmonauts and astronauts have a whole lot more in common with one another than either group has with anyone else!

7. According to Wikipedia, the Gaia hypothesis is an ecological hypothesis proposing that the biosphere and the physical components of the Earth (atmosphere, cryosphere, hydrosphere and lithosphere) are closely integrated to form a complex interacting system that maintains the climatic and biogeochemical conditions on Earth in a preferred homeostasis. Originally proposed by James Lovelock as the Earth feedback hypothesis, it was named the Gaia Hypothesis after the Greek supreme goddess of Earth. The hypothesis is frequently described as viewing the Earth as a single organism. The Gaia hypothesis was first scientifically formulated in the 1960s by the independent research scientist James Lovelock, as a consequence of his work for NASA on methods of detecting life on Mars. He initially published the *Gaia Hypothesis* in journal articles in the early 1970s followed by the popular 1979 book *Gaia: A New Look at Life on Earth*. Gaia Hypothesis, http://en.wikipedia.org/wiki/Gaia_ hypothesis, accessed 9th September 2013.

FURTHER READING

Echenoz, J. (1983), *Cherokee*, Paris: Les Editions de Minuit.
Lovelock, J. (1979), *Gaia: A New Look at Life on Earth*, Oxford: Oxford University Press.
Ward, P. (2007), *Life as We Do Not Know It*, New York: Penguin.
Ward, P., and Brownlee, D. (2003), *Rare Earth*, New York: Springer.

8 PROTOTOPIA: CRAFT, TYPE AND UTOPIA IN HISTORICAL PERSPECTIVE

FREDERIC J. SCHWARTZ

Theodor Adorno (1967: 104) began his extraordinary lecture 'Functionalism To-day' of 1965 with a disingenuous disclaimer: 'I have serious doubts as to whether I really have the right to speak before you. *Métier*, expertise in matters of craft and technique, counts for a great deal in your circle, and rightly so.'[1] His own métier, Adorno said, was music. It is, perhaps, a topos, or commonplace, but one I feel strongly about in this context. My métier is that of the historian, and not a historian of craft, but more of art, architecture and a certain strain of critical thought. Within the parameters of this problem—a historian writing about craft, and moreover a historian talking about this in the future tense—I can really only do two things. The first is to give a historical account of certain thoughts about craft and its most utopian futures—futures now past; the second is not to avoid but instead to attend to and thematize the problem of a historian thinking about the future. I will be doing this as a way of trying to get to grips with what the problem of the prototype can offer thinking about things in general.

The first thing we can say is that the constellation presented here—the proto-type as craft in the future tense—is a compelling one: things made for a better future, for the use of all. In the futurity of this set of ideas, its hope for a better world, its attempts to use the modern means of production for the modern sub-ject (the masses), it is a distinctly modernist constellation. There is one element, however, which just does not fit: that of *craft*, which seems to hark back to a mode of production, a set of skills, a social organization of makers that preceded modernity. To this, however, one can make more than one objection. Here are two. Firstly, craft as premodern has its abundant, concrete, real alibis, but it is as much a way of thinking as a historical fact. Certainly, theorists of the change of forms of production had identified the move from craft to industrial produc-tion as a radical rupture with the past—Marx, Karl Bücher, Ferdinand Tönnies and others.[2] But already before this, another rupture was described around this issue, one that did not simply involve the machine but the social relations and organizations in which craft was embedded: the guild system. With the dissolution of the guilds in the French Revolution, voices were raised that described the loss of privilege of the craftsman and related it to a loss of skills, secrets and traditions; the machine came later. Similarly, there was a change in habits of consumption, described beautifully by Sigfried Giedion (1948)—again, a change that predated the arrival of the machine. The crafts were a locus of perceived crisis in relation to social changes before any wholesale change in the technology of production. Thus, the antithesis between craft and modernity was a symptom of a change in the sense of time and thus a change in the notion of modernity, just as much as it was a change in brute facts of production. In this sense, the antithesis is as much a historical trope as it is a historical fact. Secondly, Glenn Adamson (2007) has compellingly described another aspect of this opposition, showing that the relationship of these concepts is governed less by antithesis than by symbiosis. He argues that craft bears, in Derridean terms, a 'supplemental' relation to the modernist notion of art, consistently subordinated, but in fact so insistently subordinated that one soon realizes that the very idea of the modernist (autonomous, free, masculine, ideal) depends on the idea of craft (subordinate, subject to law, feminine); it is in many ways the cart that draws the mythical horse of the modern. What this means is this: in seeing in craft a foreign body or an irritant within the logic of the modern, we have to accept that maybe the problem is not craft itself but rather modernism, the way that set of ideas cohered and is ultimately inadequate as an explanatory and organizing category. To extend the metaphor, it is less an irritant than an allergen—an innocent element that sets off a revealingly disproportionate defensive reaction.

So craft, perhaps, should not frighten us so much, and its connection to utopias gives it some modernist credentials. Consider the most compelling of these utopias, those of John Ruskin and William Morris. Their politics are quite different, but they share—all complexities, especially in the case of Morris, aside—an influential and convincing ontology of craft (Ruskin 1853; Thompson 1976). Craft here is not so much a specific set of skills or a specific mode of production but the interaction between human and material, one that is paradigmatic of the creative encounter. A craftsperson not only forms the object, but in forming the object from beginning to end, finds his or her own human creativity and potential. It is the bond between the maker and the whole product that makes the maker him or herself whole. Breaking this bond alienates labour, and it alienates man. In Ruskin's words:

> We have much studied and much perfected, of late, the great civilised invention of the division of labour; only we give it a false name. It is not, truly speaking, the labour that is divided, but the men:—divided into mere

segments of men—broken into small fragments and crumbs of life; so that all the little piece of intelligence that is left in a man is not enough to make a pin, or a nail, but exhausts itself in making the point of a pin, or the head of a nail. (1853: 165)

But pins, and nails, and indeed most other objects of human design and industry would continue to be made by the means Ruskin decried; the forces of capitalism and rationalization, the forces of modernity, had a momentum that was difficult to halt. Morris knew this, of course, calling his utopian novel of 1890 *News from Nowhere*, a book describing his utopian, socialist vision of a life free from alienation. And we recognize the unviability of this utopia in its static nature. If the utopia of craft must be craft in the future tense, this fails. Craft points beyond itself to the human subject, defined as *homo faber*—but the whole process remains tied to the phenomenology of hand production. It produces itself only as it happens and transmits its blessings in real time. Even at its best, it is craft in the *present* tense.

In his *Spirit of Utopia* of 1918, the philosopher Ernst Bloch sets out on a similar path. The first section of the book is about the applied arts; it is called 'The Production of Ornament' and, with heightened Ruskinian rhetoric, describes ornament as the surplus, the excess that harbours the energy that strives for a better world and that emerges from creative labour. In the modern age, however, 'we are poor, we have unlearned (*verlernt*) how to play . . . the hand has unlearned how to tinker, to craft (*hat das Basteln verlernt*)' (Bloch 1964: 20). It is the famous Rhine-Franconian *Bartmannskrug* or 'bearded-man pitcher' that he describes, specifically privileging the rougher versions: 'They have been imitated often. That's not a problem . . . But whoever loves them recognises how superficial the expensive [copied] pitchers are and prefers the brown, clumsy object' (Bloch 1918: 13). Of course, in this scenario, the prototype does not yet exist: it is more an ur-type that retains its authenticity, its privilege and is ruined by repetition.[3] Bloch flirts with the romantic anticapitalist notion of the everyday object, in its form, simultaneously expressing and summoning the unity of spirit of a people, invoking Alois Riegl by coyly suggesting that the object he describes is Late Roman and by discussing the utopian energy of works such as the *Kunstwollen* (Schwartz 1996). And he goes beyond the present of craft, temporally locked in the reciprocal logic of its production of subject and object, to a notion of reception that brings the future into the equation. Reception mirrors production; the encounter with the object, already fully formed, bears the potential of future self-encounter for the subject not yet fully formed or realized.

But by the second edition of his book in 1923—after the demise of expressionism, the failure of revolutionary hopes in the West in the wake of the First World

War and his own conversion to Marxism—things had changed.[4] The old pitcher remained at the beginning of his great work, but the craft it represents disappears as a viable form of human practice. It is neither superseded nor deferred. Instead, the historical possibilities of production cleave, are sundered about this point, turning craft into a fulcrum separating the two forms of production that will succeed it. On the one hand is the mass production of the machine, now drained of its spiritual energy, one which can be properly used as a lowest common denominator of production for the most mundane of uses. Indeed, to be honest and effective, it must resist the taint of cultural ambition, which it will inevitably corrupt. The energies of ornament, of excess and utopia are now to be freed from the object of use into a realm of art that can harbour at a higher potential the roughness, the imperfections, the humanity that formerly characterized craft. Craft has no future tense; pushed forward by the machine, the energies of utopia have migrated into a purified realm of art. Craft was the future of the past.

But neither Ruskin nor Bloch use the notion of the type—an idea that helps us close in on the prototype, and moreover one that is associated with utopias of production and design that we should take seriously. Le Corbusier's thinking around the 'object-type' and the 'standard' has a utopian tinge and was developed within the discussions around mass production that are implicit in the notion of the 'prototype'. For Le Corbusier and his partner in Purism, Amédée Ozenfant, standards, or types, developed toward a state of perfection of form and purpose. Where needs were by and large uniform, the objects that served them became standardized. The wine bottle, the English pipe, the café glass, the Thonet café chair, had evolved into a state of perfection that reflected perfectly the needs they served, the method of manufacture and purity of form that made them objects of culture as much as use. They called this 'mechanical selection' in which:

> [t]he respect for the laws of physics and of economy has in every age created highly selected objects . . . these objects contain analogous mathematical curves with deep resonances . . . and . . . consequently, there thus reigns a total harmony, bringing together the only two things that interest the human being: himself and what he makes. (Harrison and Wood 1992: 239)

It is an appealing and convincing idea. One might be bothered, however, by two things. Perhaps the classical rhetoric of perfection of form as an autonomous quality is too restrictive; some of the finest mass-produced products play havoc with the classical, and they of course had their own prototypes. The normative aspect of this kind of thought is problematic, but then it is, to an extent, inherent in the notion of both type and prototype. And as a historian, I am interested in the process of the retrospective conferral of the status of the 'classic', once history has stripped an object and the design process of their accidents and contingencies. In this light, such normativity seems more a phantom of a way of thinking, indeed of a valid form of cultural memory, than a threat. But there are problems of a historical kind here that we should consider. For Le Corbusier, the development of a type was no peaceful matter of purely artistic or intellectual advance. It was instead the result of violent battle; he saw the emergence of the type as subtractive, not additive, as the result of a Darwinian fight that weeded out unviable solutions. The marketplace was one example of the field across which this 'mechanical selection' took place (1987: 76); the battlefield was the other. 'The War,' he wrote in 1924:

> was the insatiable client, never satisfied, always demanding something better. The orders were to succeed and death implacable followed error. So we can say that the airplane mobilized invention, intelligence, and daring: *imagination* and *cool reason*. The same spirit built the Parthenon. (Le Corbusier 2007: 161)

As a heuristic and analytical tool, the idea of 'mechanical selection' has a certain logic (although it ignores something the military historian would insist on mentioning: the reciprocal development of battlefield technology and tactics, where the latter can very quickly reverse advances in the former). This theory is more problematic for the designer, for the maker of the prototype, the type in the future tense. In this light, it emerges that the type, as defined by Le Corbusier, is a two-edged sword, bearing both a utopian and a dystopian side. Philosophically, the historical development of the type might be seen as a realm of freedom in which the mind can reflect on its products and push them towards perfection; or it can be seen as the result of a brutal reduction, a development of the standard as the identical result of domination, of necessity. Or historically, we can say that the development of the type can be seen only retrospectively and not, *qua* type, driven prospectively. The type is identified empirically and inductively; to posit a prototype involves a sort of logical *deduction*, the statement that a design solution must necessarily follow from a set of premises. Of course, the work of prototyping more properly takes more the form of a logical *proposition*. But the notion of the prototype is somehow a misnomer, a word that contains within itself a confusion of induction and deduction. And to confuse the two is dangerous. For example as much as we might accept the basic logic of evolution in natural history, to turn this into policy or politics is fallacious; it leads to all the problems that might come to mind under the rubric of Social Darwinism. And the practical projection of various utopias of the twentieth century into the future has led to some of its worst violence, although they were based on incisive historical analyses. Thus for me, the very notion of the 'prototype', driving toward the future but caught in a fundamentally retrospective logic, is deeply problematic, utterly contradictory, an aporia. Perhaps this is behind the so-called *Bilderverbot*, or proscription on graven images, that prevented philosophers such as Adorno (1997: 22, 104, 280) from describing their utopias, though his negative dialectic was driven by a radical insistence on and performance of freedom. But that is of little use to the craftsperson or designer of prototypes. They must design, and they are entitled to hopes, dreams and a programme of human progress. For this reason, we have to find a modus operandi that can accommodate the logical and temporal conundrum of the prototype. If the title of the conference tells us that the prototype represents craft in the future tense, I would like to suggest that, at some level, we ought to modify this. Involving the necessity of thinking historically before the fact, the prototype is, we should say, craft in the *future perfect* tense. The prototyper has the task of creating *that which will have been* a type.

But let us return to Earth, to the facts. Perhaps the later Heidegger (1971) helps here, specifically his lecture 'The Thing'.[5] Heidegger distinguishes between mere 'objects' and proper 'things'. An 'object' is a physical entity in the world as it is represented to the mind, subject to the fundamentally external concerns and logic of the subject. Subordinated to the demands of the human, mere matter taken as 'ready-to-hand' rather than something with its own life (as it were), the object does not reveal itself or the nature of its being. What is this being? Heidegger's example is the jug; its being is holding, giving (the German for 'pour' and 'give' is the same: *schenken*). The giving and pouring of water or wine unites the sky and the earth; the gift of the pouring for mortals is also a 'gush' (*Guß*), etymologically an offering or sacrifice, which thus gathers together mortals and the gods. The jug thus gathers together the elements of what Heidegger calls the 'fourfold' (*das Geviert*). And here is the philosopher's answer. He makes much of the etymology of the 'thing' from the Old High German *Thing* or *dinc*, 'a gathering to deliberate on a matter under discussion, a contested matter' (1971: 172). The word still exists in Icelandic—*þing*—and indeed in Swedish, *Tingsrätt* still means a district court. So the proper 'thing' is something that gathers and unites the fourfold and in 'thinging' reveals this fundament of being to those who can attend to its thingness.

Of course, many find Heidegger's thought deeply problematic in its tendency to bracket out the social, a political problem confounded by the philosopher's own problems dealing with the history of which he was a part. But I have often been struck by the strange fact that many thinkers of architecture and design have found him to be very productive indeed and have been able to make a

politics out of his analyses (Schwartz 2009). And it is precisely Heidegger's notion of the 'thing' that has served this purpose for the last thinker of the thing
that I will invoke: Bruno Latour. In his 'Actor-Network Theory' (2005) and in
an exhibition with Peter Weibel called *Making Things Public*, Latour develops an
appealing politics of the thing (Latour and Weibel 2005). Like Heidegger, the
'thing' for Latour is not the dead matter studied by the natural sciences; instead,
it is a matter of concern, each object a locus that 'gathers around itself a different assembly of relevant parties . . . [that] triggers new occasions to passionately
differ and dispute' (Latour and Weibel 2005: 15). Objects create the public,
punctually and flexibly. Following Heidegger, he moves from phantom 'matters
of fact' to concrete, political 'matters of concern' (Latour and Weibel 2005: 19).
In an age beyond ideologies, beyond a priori political positions and projects,
politics can best happen in the gathering around the thing of concern—ad hoc,
concrete, a way of bringing people together. It is what he calls an 'object-oriented
democracy' (Latour and Weibel 2005: 16), a politics of the real that is also a
postideological utopia of the object.

What Latour describes does in fact happen. Adolf Loos, for example, put his
architecture knowingly in the public domain, made his works matters of concern, knew how to choreograph design practice and public debate as an elaborate
tango. When building authorities in Vienna halted construction on his *Haus am
Michaelerplatz* in Vienna out of fear that the building's façade would be completed without ornament, Loos embarked on a publicity campaign, giving lec-
tures, publishing articles, naming and shaming local officials who were not acting
in the public good. In general, Loos worked in the public eye and knew how to
focus widespread attention on his work (Schwartz 2012). But such strategies
failed spectacularly as often as they succeeded, and this reveals the problems with
Latour's ideas. There are two. Firstly, such 'things that talk' end up subordinating
politics to the logic of the thing or matter of concern, to the complex and problematic logic of publicity and the spectacle. Loos found himself on the right side
of the public opinion formed by a commodified press from time to time but also
on the wrong side of the public. The reasons had little to do with the strength or
weakness of his case and more to do with the machinations of the press. The press
can keep one thing invisible, and it can expose and distort others. As appealing
as a politics of the thing is, no one can really propose a politics *only* of things, of
matters fundamentally subordinated to external forces. And secondly, in subject-
ing politics to the logic of the visible and of the thing, it narrows politics down
to the isolated, intransitive. Politics can no longer be transcendent, and as tired
as notions such as justice or equality are, one does not want them to be subject
to negotiation every day.

And here is where craft and design, the type and its model might help. For designers and craftspeople have never considered objects as only matters of fact, and they have never considered them as anything but functioning beyond their own brute material being. Adorno (1967: 118) once described the process of creation, of design, as 'finding an answer to the wordless question that the material and forms pose in the mute language of the thing'. This means going beyond mere functions—for functions themselves are implicated in the system of commodity production. To serve merely function is to reduce the subject to a mere function of an already existing society. And maybe it is here that craft, the skill of material, seemingly anachronistic, can help us out of the temporal bind of the prototype, a retrospective form of perfection that can be utopian or dystopian depending on the judgements of an imperfect present. What craft allows is a reconciliation of future and present by presenting a certain congruence between them.

Think of it this way. In the heroic, free stage of the present economic system, we had the figure of the inventor, who worked in freedom. Now we have Research and Development sections, perhaps a safe-haven of creative thought but nonetheless one that is instrumentalized in the service of profit. I would like to propose something in-between: the prototyper. Perhaps the prototyper does not so much solve problems as play in dialogue with the material in an open-ended process of bricolage. Now, bricolage is not only a matter of production—though this is the word, *Bastlen* in German, that Ernst Bloch used to describe the 'tinkering' of craft—but also of consumption: this is how Michel de Certeau (1984: 29–44) described the realm of freedom of the everyday, the power of use, untheorized and uncontrolled, not subject to the strategic discourse, planning and discipline of the powers that be. The irrational, nonrationalized, unperfected, not-yet of the prototyper becomes just as provisional and contingent, unpredictable and surprising as what the user finds, and in the case of an active designer *will have found.* It is creating for uses that have not yet been conceived. For all the danger of what Baudrillard (1972: 63–87) called 'the ideological generation of needs',[6] there is a utopia here, an equalizing of provisionality in the present with what the future will have found there.

As abstract as this may be, it seems to me what is implied is the notion of the utopia of the prototype as craft in the future tense. Moreover, if we are talking about craft, bricolage and the provisionality of the prototype, it is inevitably something craftspeople and designers already know and do not need me to tell them. But it strikes me as a place where craft and design offer some sort of philosophical purchase on problems beyond them, where thinking through them can help thinking in general.

NOTES

1. A translation of Adorno's essay by Jane O. Newman and John H. Smith appears in *Oppositions*, 17 (Summer 1979), and is reprinted in Leach 1997.
2. I discuss economists' and sociologists' analyses of modernity and their engagement in discussions of the applied arts in Schwartz 1996.
3. ur-type as in original, primitive and earliest.
4. This edition has—heroically—been translated into English in Bloch 2000.
5. The essay was originally given as a lecture in 1950. This essay and the role of the thing in Heidegger's thought are discussed briefly in Harman 2005 and more extensively in Harman 2002.
6. Baudrillard refers, in fact, more broadly to the ideological 'genesis' of needs.

FURTHER READING

Adamson, G. (2007), *Thinking through Craft*, Oxford: Berg.

Adorno, T. W. (1967), 'Funktionalismus heute', in *Ohne Leitbild: Parva Aesthetica*, Frankfurt: Suhrkamp.

Adorno, T. W. (1997), *Aesthetic Theory*, trans. R. Hullot-Kentor, Minneapolis: University of Minnesota Press.

Baudrillard, J. (1972), *For a Critique of the Political Economy of the Sign*, trans. C. Levin, St Louis, MO: Telos Press.

Bloch, E. (1918), *Geist der Utopie*, 1st edn, facsimile, Frankfurt: Suhrkamp.

Bloch, E. (1964), *Geist der Utopie*, 2nd edn, Frankfurt: Suhrkamp.

Bloch, E. (2000), *The Spirit of Utopia*, trans. A. A. Nassar, Stanford, CA: Stanford University Press.

Certeau, M. de. (1984), *The Practice of Everyday Life*, trans. S. Rendall, Berkeley: University of California Press.

Giedion, S. (1948), *Mechanization Takes Command*, New York: Oxford University Press, especially the chapter 'The Nineteenth Century: Mechanization and Ruling Taste', 329–88.

Harman, G. (2002), *Tool-Being: Heidegger and the Metaphysics of Objects*, Chicago: Open Court.

Harman, G. (2005), 'Heidegger on Objects and Things', in B. Latour and P. Weibel (eds), *Making Things Public: Atmospheres of Democracy*, Karlsruhe: ZKM-Centre for Art and Media, and Cambridge, MA: MIT Press, 268–71.

Harrison, C., and Wood, P. (eds) (1992), *Art in Theory, 1900–1990: An Anthology of Changing Ideas*, Oxford: Blackwell.

Heidegger, M. (1971), 'The Thing', in *Poetry, Language, Thought*, trans. A. Hofstadter, New York: Harper and Row.

Latour, B. (2005), *Reassembling the Social: An Introduction to Actor-Network Theory*, Oxford: Oxford University Press.

Latour, B., and Weibel, P. (eds) (2005), *Making Things Public: Atmospheres of Democracy*, Karlsruhe: ZKM-Centre for Art and Media, and Cambridge, MA: MIT Press.

Leach, N. (ed.) (1997), *Rethinking Architecture: A Reader in Cultural Theory*, London: Routledge.

Le Corbusier (1987), 'Type Needs', in *The Decorative Arts of Today*, trans. J. Dunnett, Cambridge, MA: MIT Press.

Le Corbusier (2007), *Toward an Architecture*, trans. J. Goodman, Los Angeles: Getty Research Institute.

Ruskin, J. (1853), 'The Nature of Gothic', in *The Stones of Venice*, vol. 2, London: Smith, Elder.

Schwartz, F. J. (1996), *The Werkbund: Design Theory and Mass Culture before the First World War*, New Haven, CT: Yale University Press.

Schwartz, F. J. (2009), 'The Disappearing Bauhaus: Architecture and its Public in the Early Federal Republic', in J. Saletnik and R. Schuldenfrei (eds), *Bauhaus Construct: Fashioning Identity, Discourse, and Modernism*, London: Routledge.

Schwartz, F. J. (2012), 'Architecture and Crime: Adolf Loos and the Culture of the "Case"', *Art Bulletin*, vol. 94, no. 3, 409–27.

Thompson, E. P. (1976), *William Morris: Romantic to Revolutionary*, 2nd edn, New York: Pantheon.

9 PROTOTYPING FOR HIGH-VALUE, TIME-POOR USERS

STUART I. BROWN

INTRODUCTION

The extremes of a design requirement might be represented by the number of potential users. At one pole lie the mundane products, consumed in their hundreds of thousands on a daily basis: the drink bottles, disposable cups, razors and ballpoint pens. The consumer, personally unknown to the creator, could be anyone and everyone with a concomitant range of tastes, expectations and needs. At the opposite pole lie the patrons of the acclaimed artisan: frequently wealthy, possibly ostentatious, commissioning bespoke one-offs for a singular purpose which might—or might not—be practical but invariably include an unspoken but unmistakable statement of status. The educational systems of developed economies provide students with the comprehension, insights and technical skills appropriate to a profession catering for one pole or the other, whether it is a course in the design of injection mouldings for high volume manufacture or a university programme in the casting of bronze sculptures.

The client group addressed in this chapter, however, occupies a territory somewhere between these two extremes, although closer to the latter, the commissioning patron, than the former, the everyday user of everyday things. They are the expert users and consumers of high-quality goods and services, the well-heeled, time-impoverished professionals with high expectations of both form and function, expectations which can at times be hard to anticipate and harder still to fulfil. Given the existing quality and variety of learning and instruction for students of the creative professions, what justification is there for directing specific attention to this limited clientele?

An example of the creative and economic potential within the high-value market is the history of the automotive airbag restraint system: in 1980 it arrived in Europe on the prestigious Mercedes Benz S-Class saloon; by 1994 it was available on middle-of-the-range German saloons in the form of the Audi 80 and 100 models (Oswald 2001), and now it is available, as standard, on the most basic Ford, the Ka (Ford 2010). This provides a classic example of technology descending from aspirational brands towards commodity items, eventually providing a product or service to the majority of the exposure audience. The economic advantage, be it to the broad economy or simply to the balance sheet of a small employer, is that the aspirational, prestige products into which so much design effort is poured at the outset produce both a worthwhile profit in their own right and a sound design upon which more lowly products can be based as the market evolves. Of course, the process is a continuous stream, and doubtless some features appearing in today's prestige marques will be commonplace in a decade or two; there is a constant flow of products which start with an intense design endeavour for a select clientele and continue to carry their inherent value down the aspiration ladder.

This chapter provides a discussion of the design and development of high-value goods for time-impoverished, demanding consumers, using examples from the author's experience to illustrate the issues, particularly in its reference to surgical instruments. It is argued that prototyping must necessarily take a different form, centred on the users' strengths and weaknesses. As with most case studies, some of the lessons learned are of dubious value outside their sphere of origin, but it is hoped that a worthwhile proportion of these insights provide designers in other disciplines with inspiration in the difficult task of communicating with their clients.

THE ROLE OF THE COMPUTER

The foremost generator of value in many contemporary engineered products is the computer; the massive growth of computerization in the manufacturing industries since the 1980s has promoted vast improvements to the tools of design and prototype creation and consequently immense improvements in production technology. Many previously complex and invariably tedious creation processes, essential to the eventual success of the product, have thus been greatly simplified, freeing the designer's intellect to add greater value and innovation to the final artefact. The results are frequently seen in the greater quality of mass-produced items; for example, computer simulations of collapsing structures result in greater crashworthiness of motor vehicles. These are facets of a product which lend themselves to quantification and objective analysis through the physical sciences and the influence of computerization in the product cycle, which is easy to identify and results in immediate benefits for the consumer. This capability of computer-aided engineering (CAE) has had a profound influence on the notion of prototyping, particularly at an early stage of product development. The prototype consists simply of the designer's three-dimensional computer model, which moves seamlessly from the design software (CAD, or computer-aided design) to adjuvant analytical software where the digital equivalent of crash testing or wind tunnel testing is performed, usually in a process of hours or even minutes. As with old-fashioned engineering prototyping activity, the process is iterative, with many models crashed or flown before the final, highly developed version is selected. This is prototyping in its most analytical, engineering sense, sometimes pretentiously described as *in silico*, where the tools of design and the tools of analysis merge so seamlessly that the distinction between prototyping and designing is blurred.

Computation provides a similar role in the creation of value in the medical device and implant industries, and there is significant effort expended in the generation of virtual environments in which to evaluate digital prototypes. The role of the computer in the design of hip prostheses provides an insightful example, especially because the bone receiving the implant reacts dynamically, changing shape and strength as it grows to accept loads imposed by the embedded metallic components. Thus, the design method contains two iterating processes: one spatial—the successive geometries generated by the designer, and one temporal—a time series of bony adaptations to the loadings imposed by each potential implant design. Such a process goes beyond simply supplanting a traditional prototyping activity; it provides a development tool which was hitherto impossible (e.g. Jaecques, Van Oosterwyck, Muraru, Van Cleynenbreugel, De Smet, Wevers, Naert and Vander Sloten 2004; Scannell and Prendergast 2009).

There are also some limited uses of CAE to assist the designer in developing some of the less tangible and more esoteric perceptions about a product: weight and density data delivered automatically from the software can be used to predict a sense of balance in a handheld instrument; rendering and lighting effects can be used to explore the appearance of different surface finishes, and so on. However, the analytical power of CAE is ultimately of only limited value in predicting a product's interactions with its user. Alternative strategies in the design evolution need to be employed to ensure that the product meets users' more subjective expectations. It is suggested that the high-value user's expectations of the intangible and subjective properties of a product are *more* important in aspirational or high-value products intended for the professional user, since it is these clients who are likely to consider themselves as discerning buyers whose purchases reflect their intellectual calibre and social status. And, in many instances, identifying precisely what these aspirations are can be demanding.

IMPOVERISHED COLLABORATION

To ensure that these high expectations of the purchaser are met, communication with the designer needs to be strong. However, we have already asserted that this client group, who are referred to as 'high-value users' hereafter, is frequently characterized as being time-poor, committed to demanding professions and unable to devote significant time and attention to extra projects—such as collaborating with a designer to produce a new device. A conundrum therefore exists: the highly performing product which they seek requires significant input from them to ensure that it matches their needs and expectations, but their busy lives do not afford them the luxury of contributing significantly to the design process.

Occasionally this conundrum may be resolved by a particular individual in the client group who expresses an above-average interest in creating new products and purposefully assigns significant time and effort to collaborating with a design team; it becomes his or her pet project. If this occurs, it does much to resolve the conundrum described above, but it presents two particular problems: (a) such encounters between designer and user may be serendipitous and cannot be relied upon in every project; (b) the design becomes excessively influenced by one individual's preferences, endangering its broader appeal to others.

In some industries, the tension between high performance expectations and impoverished collaborative opportunities with the end user is addressed by employing surrogates of that user group: test pilots are a particular example. The average airline pilot may not be closely involved in the development of a Boeing or an Airbus, but users' needs will be expressly represented by the manufacturer's test pilots, who will fly both computer-simulated and real prototype aircraft. On the whole, this arrangement works well for a number of reasons, including the high level of objectivity in the specification of the design and the mandatory standardization of practice across the industry. The new aircraft is unlikely to contain any unpleasant surprises for its new crew.

Such 'test flying' opportunities in surgery and medicine are currently quite limited; the highly complex and varying environment in which the product performs can rarely be simulated digitally with great realism, and stringent ethical constraints prevent the testing of prototypes in patients at least until an appropriate research programme has reached an advanced stage. However, as simulation packages and the interfaces between users and computers become more complex, the possibility of digital simulation will undoubtedly open up, and the possibility of 'test flying' medical products in a simulator by 'test pilots' will become increasingly viable. An example of what is currently viable is the creation of bespoke plates for the repair of cranial defects: the modelled metal plate can be test-fitted to a model of the cranium (derived from preoperative image data) in a simulation prior to execution of the definitive surgery (Spetzger, Vougioukas and Schipper 2010).

RESOLVING THE CONUNDRUM

In the case of our high-value users, the designer should embark on a new project by respecting the two basic principles described above in the context of the airline industry: the need for a good specification and the use of accepted (or mandatory) codes for standardization. Whilst the specification should, of course, identify any known quantifiable variables, it should list any more esoteric or personal issues. The author's recent experience with surgical instruments has, for example, identified that one particular chief executive has a distaste for black polymers, and many surgeons have expressed a desire for an audible click to accompany the ratcheting function seen in many retractors and graspers.

The tension described in the previous section between expectation and collaborative opportunity is, fortunately, only one side of the story: high-value users often present other assets on which the designer and prototyper can capitalize in order to develop their product and assess its impact. The users have often gained their prestige position in society by articulating their ambitions, and this yields their first strength: their willingness to express an opinion. This is invariably tied to an above-average ability to communicate, at least concerning issues relating to their profession, including abstract scenarios and requirements. Finally, high-value users may often possess a powerful intellect, either in terms of a conventional education (which is certainly the case with surgeons) or acquired through the daily demands of the role they play in society and amongst their peers. Their intellect may manifest itself in a number of ways, including a broad knowledge of facts, events, precedents and principles and an appreciation of the potential in ideas which are at early stage of development.

It is these characteristics of high-value users which make them particularly adept at performing thought experiments—applying prior experience and knowledge to explore what-if scenarios and reach a credible and justifiable conclusion. The thought experiment can (and should) possess all the essential elements of the conventional scientific method—a hypothesis, a method for evaluating the hypothesis (as free as possible from bias) and the critical judgement of results and their significance—performed entirely conceptually. This is particularly true in medicine: the practical, financial and ethical difficulties in performing research mean that many projects (be it to establish a diagnosis in an individual patient or to undertake a full-scale investigation of a complex disease) commence by applying the physician's huge range of taught and experiential knowledge to problem-solving at a hypothetical level before reaching for the scalpel or completing the research-funding proposal. The thought experiment, therefore, will not be an alien exercise to many potential clients. Thus, the anticipated product can be initially evaluated simply by an imaginative discussion between designer and user of its potential form, function and likely utility, inevitably assisted by simple props exemplified by the proverbial back-of-an-envelope sketch.

Of course, conjecturing on the likely form, function, value and use of any design is a universal part of the design process and is hardly unique to the scenarios discussed here. Indeed, crafts people of all types and all disciplines undertake the same mental projection task, overtly or otherwise; their imagined response to a product is often the motivation for pursuing its creation. The difference is simply one of scale. In the high-value user context, the thought experiment may be more lively and productive, most especially because it capitalizes on the knowledge, abstract reasoning and communication skills described above in which many valued users are highly proficient. So, although the client may have little time to devote to the project, the process of fleshing out the initial concept—the mental prototype—to a stage where substantive design can proceed is rapid and efficient and may lead to a concept in which many particulars have been explored (abstractly) early in the design cycle.

There are two obvious, related forms of abstracted prototyping which such users may indulge to pursue and refine the design of a product: retrospection, the evaluation of the envisaged design in the context of some prior experience, and cross-fertilization, introducing into the imagined scenario some form or function from another discipline. In the context of surgical devices, the retrospection element is more potent than might be the case for many other modern products simply because the history of surgery reaches back to antiquity—at least to the Egyptian societies (Goodrich 2007; Harer 1994). The design of the ultramodern articulating 'DARES' needle driver for laparoscopic surgery (i.e. keyhole surgery in the abdomen), illustrated in Figure 9.1, is a case in point. The aim of the instrument is to allow the surgeon to perform suturing and knot-tying through the laparoscopic keyhole in exactly the same way as would have been hitherto accomplished manually in a conventional, open approach. The retrospection element of the DARES design drew upon well-established customs and precedence for the performance of manual surgical suturing tasks performed with a conventional open approach: the size and curved shape of the needle was known, and the trajectory through which the surgeon needed to drive the needle was understood by both designer and surgeon alike. Thus, a new instrument could be conceptualized, based on a retrospective view of suturing practice in the era before keyhole surgery, and its potential uses discussed long before any design work was undertaken. Discussions of the concept identified a requirement for a wrist-like joint near the tip of an otherwise straight and conventional instrument; this feature is evident in Figure 9.1.

Figure 9.1   The DARES articulating needle grasper with its wrist-like joint (top), and a conventional, rigid instrument (bottom). © James Gove and Duncan Martin.

The other element of this conceptual prototyping process, cross-fertilization, is a powerful tool for innovation, although it is inevitably limited to fields within protagonists' experience. Two simple examples from the author's colleagues demonstrate the value of cross-fertilization and have resulted in successful patents. The first of these relates again to the DARES needle driver mentioned above; a mechanism was required to lock the needle into the driver's jaws, allowing the surgeon's grip on the jaws to be relaxed. The mechanism implemented in the completed design was drawn from prior knowledge of the way in which roof support beams used in coal mines were traditionally jammed into place using a so-called pit prop—the concept is illustrated in Figure 9.2 (Frank, Martin, Rutherford, Brown, Gove and Kelly 2006).

In the second example, a multipurpose surgical instrument was sought, which the surgeon could completely enclose within the palm of the hand when not in use. Inspiration for the design of this instrument came from the designer's prior experience in the weaving industry where scissors had been designed which could be enclosed within the weaver's hand when handling the fabric, but deployed

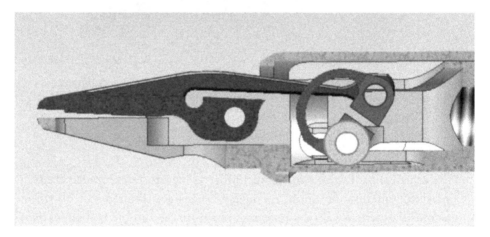

Figure 9.2   How the coal miner's pit prop inspired the locking mechanism in DARES: (top) by forcing the pit prop the mine's roof is supported. © Getty Images. (bottom) Likewise, by rotating the DARES 'pit prop', a C-shaped spring, the jaw is supported. © Duncan Martin and James Gove.

at will to cut loose threads. The design was such that the scissors were enclosed by the small and ring finger when not in use, leaving the middle finger, index finger and thumb free. The final device is shown in Figure 9.3 (Cuschieri, Frank, Brown, Martin and Gove 2003).

Note that in these latter examples, the concepts came from the designer, not the surgeon, although both were discussed in some detail with the surgeon before

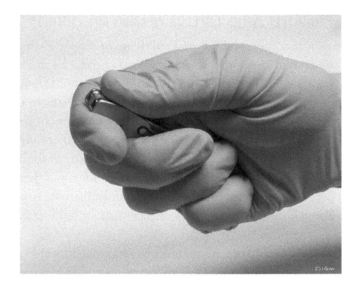

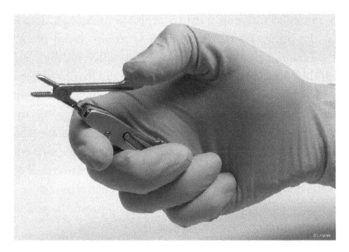

Figure 9.3 A multipurpose surgical instrument small enough to be entirely enclosed within the surgeon's hand (top) and extended for use when required (bottom). © James Gove and Stuart Brown.

reaching the substantive design stage. This illustrates the need for the designer and the user to be matched in terms of background knowledge, conceptualizing abilities and communication skills; great care must be taken that the conceptual prototype is not altered in some fundamental way because one party's grasp of the idea is different from the other party's.

CONCEPTUAL PROTOTYPE? IS THE EMPEROR WEARING ANY CLOTHES?

Is the notion of a conceptual prototype a valid one or simply a semantic excuse for failing to undertake some other skilled activity to produce a meaningful artefact? The answer is, inevitably, it depends. Firstly, no one would argue against the need for employing the full range of prototyping skills relevant to the development of any particular product; the absence of a prototype cannot be excused on the basis of 'well, we all had a big discussion about it'. Furthermore, the utility and value of conceptualization depends entirely on the ability of the designer and client to imagine new products and communicate their ideas—if there is a failure by either party to imagine or communicate proficiently, then the concept cannot find its way into a finished product, at least not without more extensive use of conventional prototyping.

However, another very pertinent question is 'what role does either party need the imagined concept to perform?' Perhaps the primary role of a prototype is to build confidence, and certainly the basic suitability of the envisaged form to accomplish the intended function must be explored in enough detail to establish confidence in the proposal. The interaction must also build the client's confidence that the designer has grasped the concept which he/she seeks to convey. In order to do this, a surgeon, for example, might say that he/she wants the new device to look, feel or perform like an existing instrument and must have complete confidence that the designer is sufficiently knowledgeable to understand the allusion. A long diversionary discussion to further elaborate what properties are being alluded to will only serve to undermine the potency of employing the allusion as a shorthand in the first place. The client must also instil confidence in the designer; the designer needs assurance that the client has a clear vision of the task the design sets out to address and is unlikely to move the goalposts at some critical stage of the project.

The role of a prototype is also to uncover likely weaknesses in the design proposal. After assessment by the client, a good, fully functioning prototype artefact should leave little room for argument about whether the design will succeed in its mission. Exploring the same questions of suitability with only a mental model to test is far more prone to error: both sides need to be honest, based on their experience, about the likelihood of success and should readily confront unknowns which threaten the design. It should be emphasized that this can be a difficult discussion if the client is a professional of status and power whose views are rarely opposed! If weaknesses in the design cannot be resolved, or even acknowledged, at this stage, then the only alternative is to build a prototype and substantiate the concern to the satisfaction of both parties.

So, is a prototype in the form of a mental concept really a valid notion? Yes, if both the client and the designer can understand the concept, express its properties, understand its role and agree on its weaknesses. If not, a more conventional approach is required.

A MORE CONVENTIONAL APPROACH

There are two particular messages concerning conventional prototyping for the high-value user. Firstly, prototyping cannot be avoided; the conceptualization activity described at length above serves to provide greater assurance that later prototyping activity is more likely to be right the first time and the number of design iterations subsequently reduced, but it cannot obviate the need for prototyping altogether. Secondly, the client is expecting an aspirational product at the end of the process and will certainly expect that the prototypes have an aspirational feel to them. Whilst the media is attracted to tales of entrepreneurs lashing together novel inventions from scrap metal and string, the reality is that nearly all valuable products will be developed in an environment which reflects their value: with care, attention and, if necessary, expense.

In the production of surgical prototypes, the starting point is always in software, usually concurrent development of a mechanical design in CAD software, an analytical design in Finite Element Analysis (FEA) software[1] and modelling of the relevant anatomy based on images acquired from Computed Tomography (CT) or Magnetic Resonance Imaging (MRI) and subsequently modified in specialized surface modelling software. The interaction of these three programs (which can often share the same file formats) serves to create an initial design which exhibits the desired functional attributes and fits into the modelled anatomy. Making full use of the visualization elements of these programs will provide a virtual reality prototype with a very high level of realism; movies can be made to illustrate assembly and use; 'ghosting' can reveal hidden internal structures, and the user can walk around the device. Making changes at this stage is straightforward, so multiple versions and iterations can be explored with little effort.

Various CAD models of a device known as the Dundee EndoCone® are shown in Figure 9.4. This is a new device from the author's team which allows abdominal surgery to be conducted through a single keyhole, located at the umbilicus (where access to the abdominal organs can be obtained relatively easily) (Cuschieri, Frank, Brown, Kelly, Rutherford, Martin and Gove 2006). During the course of development, a huge range of forms were explored in CAD, of which only a few were pursued to the stage of a physical prototype.

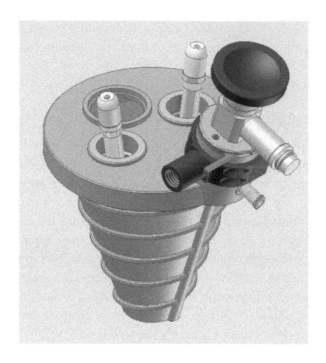

Figure 9.4   Illustration of some of the iterative concepts developed in CAD for the EndoCone®. © Timothy Frank.

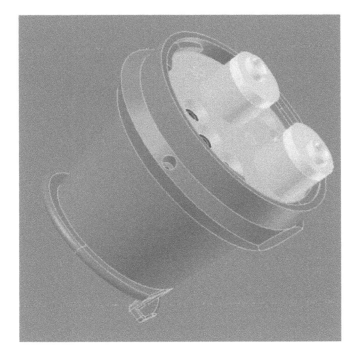

Figure 9.4   (*Continued*)

Prototyping at this stage makes further use of the CAD design, which can be downloaded directly to the machine tool for manufacture. The EndoCone® features a conical form around which is a simple helical thread, and this can be made either by a subtractive process (in this case, milling from bar stock on a five-axis milling centre) or by an additive process (Selective Laser Sintering, SLS, for example: SLS is a process in which an object is built up from successive layers of a substrate powder, with each successive layer fused to the preceding one by sintering with a computer-controlled laser). Both methods are suitable for construction in stainless steel, which was specified by the client. The additive SLS process was selected because of its availability through online service providers. It should be noted that modern additive processes (which also include stereolithography and Fused Deposition Modelling) permit the construction of forms which would be impossible with any other type of construction, and this advantage should be pursued, where appropriate, to add value to the finished product. Figure 9.5 shows the SLS EndoCone® prototype, which was hand polished to achieve the desired surface finish.

Where one of the additive processes is not directly suitable for manufacturing the prototype, it can be used for making the tooling from which the finished

(C) James Gove

Figure 9.5   The final SLS prototype of the EndoCone® in stainless steel with silicone valves.
© James Gove.

part can then be derived; for example, additive processes can be used for making casting patterns or moulds for resins. In the case of the EndoCone®, stereolithography was employed to create moulds into which two-part silicone was poured to create valve assemblies.

Prototype parts of the EndoCone® produced by SLS had sufficient integrity to permit their use in experimental surgical procedures once the relevant quality requirements had been met (as specified in this case by ISO 13485) and ethical permission obtained from the patients. The utility of the prototype is thus further extended as it becomes, in effect, the initial production hardware standard.

In the case of working with the high-value user, these additive processes provide not only realistic, attractive and usable prototypes, but they also meet another need commonly encountered with such clients—the need for instant results. The lead time from completion of the CAD file to receipt of the semifinished parts is usually just a few days, so usable prototypes of simple devices can be obtained within five to ten working days. For more complex structures, many components created initially with SLS can withstand subsequent conventional machining operations and will maintain tight tolerances, allowing product creation to be a mixture of additive and traditional, subtractive processes, albeit with a concomitant increase in lead time.

ANOTHER HIGH-VALUE USER

The term high-value user has been used throughout this chapter to indicate a high-status professional and to reflect the value they are accorded, rightly or wrongly, by society. Whilst it is hard to argue against the value of the surgical profession to society, there are plenty of other high-value users whose status would not survive egalitarian scrutiny! Conversely, there are plenty of stakeholders whose contribution to a product's value is out of proportion to the status and deference with which they are treated by society. It is likely that this is true for most, if not all, aspirational or high-value products; it is certainly true for surgical instruments.

In the case of the products developed by the author's group, one of the key stakeholders is the sterile services technician. All reusable surgical devices go through a process of cleaning, inspection, packaging and sterilization numerous times throughout their life, and these procedures are accomplished by technicians whose communication and abstract reasoning skills may be somewhat less than those of the surgeon. Nevertheless, their involvement in product development is absolutely vital, since if a product cannot be cleaned and sterilized, it cannot be used in the operating theatre. An entirely different approach to engage these stakeholders will be required, and whilst this is not discussed further in this chapter, the reader must recognize that it can be at least as important as engaging the high-status user. Society may not be egalitarian, but the designer certainly should be.

CONCLUSION

Products and services are required by users who occupy a high status in society and/or their profession, and addressing the needs of this client group can be of great importance to industry, particularly because some of the value inherent in these products eventually cascades to a wider buying public. Engaging these high-value users can be difficult if they lack the time and commitment to work with the designer, and this difficulty is amplified by the users' frequent tendency to expect exceptional standards of function and desirability in their purchases. A way to work around this collaborative deficiency is to capitalize on clients' intellectual and communication skills at the conceptual stage to create a well-defined mental model of the product before committing it to the formal design process. It is suggested that when this conceptualization is pursued to a high degree, it amounts to a form of prototyping.

The traditional interpretation of what a prototype is must not be ignored, although modern methods can make the production process simpler and still allow aesthetically and functionally pleasing results to be obtained.

Finally, simply because great effort must be expended to meet the demands of the high-status user, the needs and contribution of the low-status stakeholder must not be ignored, since their contribution can easily make or break an otherwise valuable product.

NOTE

1. Finite element analysis is a commonly used computational technique implemented through a dedicated software package for determining specific engineering properties of a design, such as stiffness, strength, hydrodynamic performance, and so on.

FURTHER READING

Cuschieri, A., Frank, T., Brown, S., Kelly, L., Rutherford, I., Martin, D., and Gove, J. (2006), *Device for Establishing Free Transcutaneous Access to an Endoscopic Surgical Area*, European Patent EP1 731 105.

Cuschieri, A., Frank, T., Brown, S., Martin, D., and Gove, J. (2003), *Medical Instrument for Hand-assisted Minimally Invasive Surgery*, European Patent EP1 329 201.

Ford (2010), 'Keeping You Safe on the Road', Ford, http://www.ford.co.uk/Cars/Ka/Safetyandsecurity, accessed 6 April 2010.

Frank, T., Martin, D., Rutherford, I., Brown, S., Gove, J., and Kelly, L. (2006), *Medical Instrument for Grasping an Object, in Particular a Needle Holder*, European Patent EP1 872 729.

Goodrich, J.T. (2007), 'Cervical Spine Surgery in the Ancient and Medieval Worlds', *Neurosurg Focus*, 23/1: E7.

Harer, W.B., Jr. (1994), 'Peseshkef: The First Special-purpose Surgical Instrument', *Obstet Gynecol*, 83/6: 1053–5.

Jaecques, S.V., Van Oosterwyck, H., Muraru, L., Van Cleynenbreugel, T., De Smet, E., Wevers, M., Naert, I., and Vander Sloten, J. (2004), 'Individualised, Micro CT-based Finite Element Modelling as a Tool for Biomechanical Analysis Related to Tissue Engineering of Bone', *Biomaterials*, 25/9: 1683–96.

Oswald, W. (2001), *Deutsche Autos 1945–1990*, vol. 4, Stuttgart: Motorbuch Verlag.

Scannell, P.T., and Prendergast, P.J. (2009), 'Cortical and Interfacial Bone Changes Around a Non-cemented Hip Implant: Simulations Using a Combined Strain/Damage Remodelling Algorithm', *Med Eng Phys*, 31/4: 477–88, http://www.ncbi.nlm.nih.gov/pubmed/19188086.

Spetzger, U., Vougioukas, V., and Schipper, J. (2010), 'Materials and Techniques for Osseous Skull Reconstruction', *Minim Invasive Ther Allied Technol*, 19/2: 110–21.

10 COMPUTER-EMBEDDED DESIGN: PAIPR PROTOTYPING

STEVE GILL

Steven Pinker once said that his worst product interaction experiences were with a Bang & Olufsen television and phone. It should worry those with an interest in design that there should be a phone in production that a Massachusetts Institute of Technology professor cannot operate, let alone one from a company known as a designer brand. Yet the problems he found here arose because both the television and the phone are computer-embedded products.

The computers in computer-embedded products are constrained and controlled in such a way as to appropriately serve the design of the product in which they are embedded. To paraphrase Bill Buxton (2001), a PC is a computer you type into, a phone is a computer you put your ear to and a digital camera is a computer you look into. Products that have computers embedded within them surround us. Increasingly, the product is actually the user interface, while what we think of as the product is largely just packaging it (think of the iPhone). Switches, dials, sliders, touchscreens, and so on occupy a middle ground, behaving as a physical conduit to our virtual experience. Some years ago the author had a conversation with an interactive appliance design expert who believed, through experience, that industrial designers tend to address user interfaces, particularly product graphical user interfaces (GUIs), with a two-dimensional mentality. Considering industrial design is focused on three-dimensional output, that is a damning criticism, but should it surprise us?

At the core of the issue, is the fact that the computers within these machines enable so many possibilities that designing them to appropriately exploit that power is the problem. Consider just how much computing power we have at our disposal in the modern era. In the mid-to late 1960s NASA developed a flight computer for the Apollo programme. Each Saturn V rocket carried two: one in the Command Module and one in the Lunar Lander. These computers had to handle radar, orbital rendezvous, navigation, engine firing and autopilot functions. They performed almost flawlessly throughout. Their specifications included 1 MHz processing speed with 1KB onboard RAM and 12KB of ROM.

These early computers were very expensive, and their functions were limited by their lack of computing power. Highly trained operators (astronauts backed up by a team of computer experts in Houston) learned to deal with their limitations. Our problem *now* is that computers are powerful, cheap and ubiquitous. The iPhone 5, for example, has 1200 times the processing speed of the Apollo computer, more than a million times the RAM and the rough equivalent of more than five million times the ROM. In order to succeed, these far more powerful machines need to be readily accessible to a nontrained, disinterested user quickly, easily and without an instruction manual. Unfortunately, they are frequently ill-conceived, largely because the design process is flawed. Much of the problem is connected to the issues designers have with creating appropriate prototypes for computer-embedded products.

When designers develop a design for a noncomputer-embedded product—for example a chair or a light—prototypes of various kinds (soft models, rigs and facsimile models) play their part in a well-ordered iterative system that ends with a well-understood product. This reflects a core recognition in the design profession that designers need to be able to make quick and dirty prototypes, employing what Schrage (1999) described as Serious Play in order to evaluate the tangible interactions of their designs early in the design process. At the end of that process, the client is able to review the design and if necessary ask for adjustments to be made.

Now consider the design process for a computer-embedded product. In this case, the designer employs soft models to test ergonomics, but much of the users' interactions are *computer* interactions. For these, a screen-based prototype is typically employed in place of the rig-based prototype. This essentially occurs because designers do not have the skills to build very complex computer-based prototypes. Unfortunately, screen-based prototypes are not very good at simulating user interactions because our physical interaction with a product has a pronounced effect on our cognition. So, while screen-based prototypes are *good* at simulating products in which we poke largely unyielding buttons on a large, flat vertical interface with our index finger, like a microwave oven (Sharp, Wright, Sharp and Petzny 1996), they are *poor* at simulating products that we grasp in our hand. Handheld products might have controls that are not on the upper surface and which may be triggers or sliders or dials, and so forth. Even in light of this, however, one might argue that employing a screen-based prototype is a pragmatic if less than optimal solution that enables a perfectly workable design process: once the industrial designer has completed their work, an electronics designer will build a fully working tangible prototype. The client is then able to review the prototype before making an informed decision on the complete design proposal. One might argue all that happens in this case is that the electronic designer has made the prototype rather than the designer. Unfortunately, the reality is quite different. Electronics designers have to deal with a lot. They need to design a reliable, workable product that can be produced to budget at the right scale without drawing on too much power and so on. They are not trained to tackle usability issues, and even if they were, producing a full working prototype takes too long and is too complex to be part of a truly iterative process.

So while commentators have continually criticized the poor computer-embedded product design process (see Buxton 2007; Cooper 2004; Loudon 2006 for examples) and while that criticism is certainly justified, this author would argue that there are not yet enough serious, detailed and connected suggestions for industrial designer-orientated methodologies that might be employed to solve the issue. Part of the problem is that these products are so remarkably complex that they require a far more holistic methodology, and this has certainly been recognized. As far back as the mid-1990s Thomas, Meech and Macredie (1995) were already arguing for a systems approach. By 2000 Hollan had developed that concept further, arguing the case for distributed cognition (Hollan, Hutchins and Kirsh 2000). But how do we empower industrial designers to undertake these approaches? A number of companies (e.g. IDEO, DCA and PDD) have developed expertise in the development of computer-embedded products and have multidisciplinary teams in-house who are able to deal with complex prototyping issues. Most designers do not have access to the same facilities or expertise, however, and recent research by Culverhouse (2012) has found that even when electronics expertise is available in-house, it is not possible to utilize it quickly and iteratively in real-world scenarios. A number of attempts have been made to tackle this issue and among them are:

> *Experience Prototyping* (Buchenau and Suri 2000), an ethnographic approach involving the use of low-tech props, role play and improvisation.
> *Wizard of Oz* simulations (Maulsby, Greenberg and Mander 1993), which involve unseen human operators simulating sophisticated machine responses.
> *Augmented Reality* (Nam and Woohan 2003), which uses a combination of real and virtual simulations.
> *Phidgets* (Greenberg and Fitchett 2001) and *Arduino* (Burleson, Jenson, Raaschou and Frohold 2007) both of which provide electronic building blocks.
> *Paper Prototyping* (Snyder 2003), a well-tested and entirely low-tech approach involving a facilitator observing user interactions and simulating

machine responses by, for example, placing drawings of screens on a model of the appliance held by the user.

Dtools (Hartmann, Abdulla, Klemmer and Mittal 2007), a toolkit with bespoke hardware and software and the first attempt to produce an integrated solution to the hardware/software prototyping problem.

All of these approaches represent real progress for the field, and some can be used in conjunction with others (generally speaking, the low-tech and high-tech methods can be used together). However, those methods that use electronics tend to focus on solving technical problems, whereas the intended users (designers) are, by and large, nontechnical.

The end result is that, in most cases, the physical prototype is not able to play its part in the iterative design development process. This means that the full interaction experience of a computer-embedded product design is not experienced until very late in the design process. Thus, while in theory, the client can ask for the project to be restarted, it does not, in fact, often happen because the time and cost of developing a design all the way to a working prototype is so significant. What happens then is that the product is either launched (flaws and all) or cancelled.

The author leads a research group called PAIPR,[1] an industrial design research group with an interest in developing methods for designers involved in the development of computer-embedded products. PAIPR concentrates on methods that are accessible to designers and which require as little as possible technological understanding. The group seeks to place the iterative prototype in its rightful place at the heart of the design process for computer-embedded products, much as it has always been for more traditional products.

At the core of one of the group's techniques is a product called an IE Unit, a low-tech product that works by facilitating the connection of a model embedded with switches to a PC-based GUI prototype (Gill 2003). The system allows the PC to receive keyboard inputs (see Figure 10.1) so that when a user activates a switch in the model, the PC responds to a perceived keyboard input and a keyboard-triggered (usually *Flash*-based) GUI is activated. This system has enabled hundreds of tangible prototypes to be produced over the years, most of them by undergraduate students learning about information ergonomics. As a result of their experiences, PAIPR has become convinced of the value of tangible prototypes and physicality. In 2008 they published research with colleagues at Lancaster University that quantified the effects of physicality on user interactions, effectively proving the importance of an early, iterative physical

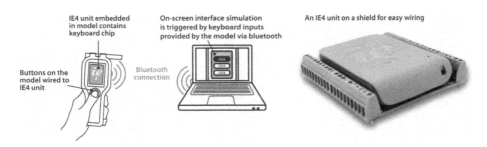

IE4 unit embedded
in model contains
keyboard chip

On-screen interface simulation
is triggered by keyboard inputs
provided by the model via bluetooth

An IE4 unit on a shield for easy wiring

Buttons on the
model wired to
IE4 unit

Bluetooth
connection

Figure 10.1   IE Unit linking a prototype to a PC (left), and a fourth-generation IE Unit with screw terminal board (right). Source: Steve Gill.

prototype-based design process (Gill, Walker, Loudon, Dix, Wooley, Ramduny-Ellis and Hare 2008).

One aspect of the *IE System* in this form is that the GUI is displayed on a remote PC screen. PAIPR wished to explore:

> Whether a tangible prototype, even one with limitations (e.g. a discrete screen), was more similar to a final product than the now traditional monitor-based prototypes most commonly used by industry.
>
> How *quick* or how *dirty* can the prototyping process be and still provide valuable feedback early in the design process, that is the level of fidelity required to obtain an acceptable degree of tangible accuracy.

A BT *Equinox* phone was reverse engineered to mimic a very high-fidelity tangible prototype. Genuine *Equinox* mouldings housed a second-generation *IE Unit*, and a representation of the screen's output was displayed on a PC monitor via a *Flash* GUI. The same Flash interface was used as the basis of a full on-screen prototype, which would be interacted with through a touchscreen. This was referred to this as the *software* prototype.

A test programme was designed to compare the performance of a real *Equinox* phone, the *IE Unit* prototype and the *Software* prototype (see Figure 10.2). Tasks were chosen to include common functions (ranging from simple to complex), unusual functions (such as the *Equinox*'s SMS button) and functions that involved more than straightforward transitions between the product's states. Seventy-nine participants were divided into three independent groups (one for each manifestation of the interface, i.e. *Equinox*, *IE Unit* and *Software*) and given a series of tasks, each of which was timed and graded.

Figure 10.2   *Equinox* prototypes (from left to right): low fidelity (Sketch), high fidelity (IE Unit), real product (*Equinox*) and touchscreen (Software). Source: Steve Gill.

The data demonstrated that the *Equinox* and the physical prototype performed in a more similar fashion than the software alone. This was especially true of the time taken to complete each task (see Figure 10.3), but in performance, the software was never better than the tangible prototype and sometimes markedly worse. In Norman's theory (1988), the system image created by the physical prototype is a better fit with the user's mental model of a phone device than a purely software simulation. This result is all the more significant for two major factors:

1. A phone is a ubiquitous computer-embedded product, so everyone in the test was able to draw on previous experience.
2. The *Equinox* has an all-push button interface with controls mounted on the top surface. This allows the software prototype to compete on favourable terms. Had the selected appliance featured sliders, dials, triggers, and so on, or had the controls been mounted in a more three-dimensional fashion around the product, then the software simulation may have matched the performance of the real product even less.

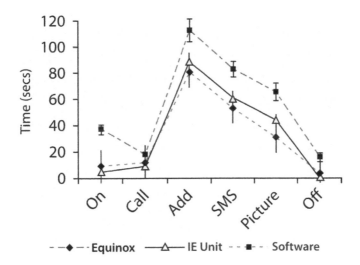

Figure 10.3 Time taken for each phone task. Bars are standard error. Source: Steve Gill.

The data demonstrated that at high fidelity levels, a relatively quickly built, low-tech prototype will outperform the standard screen-based industry method of simulation. What was so far unclear was how much effect the physical interaction was having on the user. In other words, could a very low-fidelity physical prototype and interface give useful results in the same or less time than an entirely screen-based prototype? To find out, an ultra-low-fidelity physical prototype was constructed and married to a low-fidelity GUI. The new prototype was constructed in blue modelling foam with the switches being topped with card cut-outs in the shape of the switches on the real phone. On top of these were glued the button graphics, and the screen was represented by a piece of coloured paper. The new *Flash* GUI was created using sketch work produced on-screen via the mouse. The GUI was driven via keystrokes in the same way as the higher fidelity prototype described above.

Further tests were now carried out using the low-fidelity (*Sketch*) prototype and using a similar procedure to the first experiment but without the *SMS* and *Add* tasks.

The low-fidelity *Sketch* prototype had very similar results to the high-fidelity *IE Unit* prototype in both time (see Figure 10.4) and performance, thus demonstrating the importance of the tangible prototype. The significance of the results lies in the fact that more accurate results were produced from a quicker, dirtier, tangible prototype produced in 80 per cent less time than the high-fidelity screen-based interface.

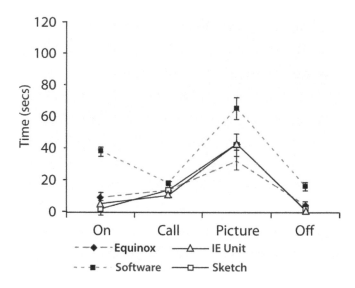

Figure 10.4 Time taken to complete phone tasks on Sketch prototype versus other prototypes and *Equinox*. Source: Steve Gill.

LOOKING FORWARD

The research described above, backed by studies of the challenges designers face (Gill, Loudon and Walker 2008) and the work carried out with industry (Gill 2009) has given PAIPR the material to produce a set of guidelines to direct future research on prototyping methodologies. These include:

SPEED AND FIT

A successful computer-embedded product prototyping system must provide a good fit for the way designers already work. To achieve this, toolkits need to enable fast, iterative, low-fidelity prototyping in two hours or less without electronics or programming knowledge.

CAPABILITY

Modern computer-embedded products require many input possibilities. Prototyping toolkits need to enable a wide range (25–50) of varied input types, including touch screen and analogue controls (dials, sliders, etc.) as well as digital inputs (e.g. push buttons and rotary switches). For full flexibility, systems should ideally be capable of utilizing off-the-shelf components.

PHYSICALITY AND SCALE

The proven importance of physicality in computer-embedded product interactions directly implies an importance of scale. Thus, for example, a digital camera prototype at one and a half times the size of the intended product (to make prototyping easier) will have very different physicality from the finished product. It will therefore probably also have different user interactions. It follows that a successful prototyping method should enable 1:1 scaling.

SCREENS

There are some applications where the inclusion of the screen is required. In general, the rule of thumb is that 'eyes down' activities, such as mobile phone texting, require a screen on the prototype, whereas 'eyes up' activities, such as navigating menus, do not.

EDUCATION

If designers are to reclaim their role as prototype-led innovators and user champions in the computer-embedded product field, then design courses need to train students accordingly.

Using these guidelines and others, PAIPR have been looking at improving their approach. A very brief description of some of that work is detailed below.

VERY RAPID ITERATIVE PROTOTYPING

One of the guidelines above states that interactive, tangible low-fidelity prototypes need to be producible in two hours or less. One of PAIPR's members, Culverhouse, worked on a method of achieving this (Culverhouse and Gill 2009). He has proposed a system called StickIT that exploits the properties of passive radio frequency identification (RFID) tags. The tags are activated by a switch so that they can only be detected when the switch is closed. A conductive substrate and coaxial pin system borrowed from Lancaster University's *Voodoo10* ad hoc networking system (Villar and Gellerson 2007) is used to allow the RFIDs to share a single aerial. A reader is mounted on a glove so that, in a handheld device, it is always close enough to the RFID tag to power it up. Meanwhile, a Bluetooth transmitter on the glove sends a translated keyboard input to the PC, which can be used to trigger changes in the GUI (Figure 10.5). The system allows the switches to be moved anywhere on the surface without any wiring or power issues. Switches can also be added or removed very easily.

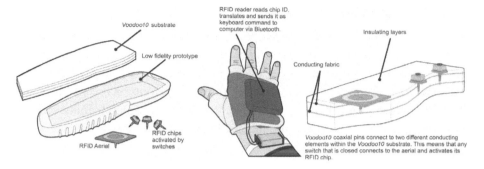

Figure 10.5   The StickIT prototyping method.

BALANCING PHYSICALITY AND FIDELITY

The importance of tangible prototypes and the advantage they enjoy over virtual prototypes was discussed earlier in the chapter. One of the interesting aspects of that research that was not mentioned in detail for space reasons was that when the fidelity of the prototype dropped below a certain level, the performance of the tangible prototype decreased markedly. This led to an important question: 'How low can the fidelity of a tangible prototype be taken before the data produced from user tests upon it become unrepresentative of the performance of the final product?'

Another PAIPR member, Hare, led a study that set out to answer this question (Hare, Gill, Loudon, Ramduny-Ellis and Dix 2009). Time was used to govern fidelity, and so Hare was tasked with creating three prototypes. She was given one hour to make the first, one day to make the second and one week to make the third. User tests were carried out on the resulting prototypes. What was found was more evidence that physicality is important. What was *not* found was a clear and present link between the level of fidelity and the accuracy of user experience; this is an area that PAIPR are consequently examining this in more depth.

NEW PARADIGMS

One of the current aims of PAIPR is to develop a tangible prototyping system so fast and flexible that it allows designers to develop new interaction paradigms for technologies that do not yet exist. This is a work in progress. However, one of the early bonuses of the programme was a technique to maintain physicality while gaining the advantage of mounting a screen on the prototype without the scale, power, speed and technological issues that accompany such an inclusion. The researcher, Zampelis, spotted the potential for the *AR Toolkit* to simulate an

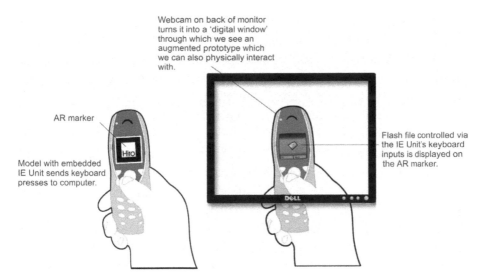

Webcam on back of monitor turns it into a 'digital window' through which we see an augmented prototype which we can also physically interact with.

AR marker

Model with embedded IE Unit sends keyboard presses to computer.

Flash file controlled via the IE Unit's keyboard inputs is displayed on the AR marker.

Figure 10.6   IRIS.

embedded screen. Zampelis moved the camera to the rear of the screen so that any object with the appropriate barcode that was held behind it showed on the screen with the virtual display projected on its surface. The resulting system is called IRIS (Figure 10.6) and allows the user to both feel and see the device while the augmented reality (AR) aspect meant the screen appeared on the appliance. Zampelis modified the AR software so that IRIS works with keyboard-triggered Flash files. Consequently, it works with both the *IE System* and StickIT.

CONCLUSIONS

Industrial designers have always valued prototypes because they know that they enable better products that produce a satisfactory end user experience. Computer-embedded products have been with us for some time, but the problems of developing them using appropriate, designer-friendly, quick and dirty tangible prototyping methods have not been, as yet, fully resolved. As well as a host of techniques developed by researchers and practitioners across the world, a common solution has been to use multidisciplinary teams to design computer-embedded products. Recent research by PAIPR has found a significant issue with this theoretically sound practice, namely that aligning the availabilities of the various skill sets in the context of more than a single project is somewhat problematic. Another common solution is to prototype virtually by using touchscreen mock-ups of product interfaces. This too is problematic.

PAIPR has empirically demonstrated what has long been qualitatively recognized—a tangible prototype has a significant effect on the interactions of a user. Critically, the research has demonstrated that the physical prototype better mimics the interactions of a real product than the touchscreen alone. This continues to be the case even when the fidelity of both the tangible prototype and its interface are dropped significantly. This makes a lot of sense because it has been understood for many years that we do not experience the world through a series of separate channels as was once thought. In fact, our senses all operate together, and it is sometimes difficult for us to know which one is telling us what. The *McGurk Effect* is a good example of this. As far back as 1978, McGurk and McDonald proved that lip reading can actually change what we hear a person say. Even when we know the person is making one sound, we cannot prevent ourselves hearing another sound if we watch the person mouth the movements of another sound. This is because the world we perceive is as much about what we do with information as the information itself. In that context, it makes perfect sense that a tangible prototype is going to affect our interactions in a way that might not at first seem logical. It follows that in order to design effectively, designers need to continue to use prototypes in the way they traditionally have and that computer-embedded products need them no less than any other kind of product. In some ways, one could argue, computer-embedded products need tangible prototyping methods more than most other products by dint of the sheer complexity of the user interactions they enable.

Since creating multidisciplinary teams does not necessarily solve the problem of enabling tangible prototypes, it follows that designers need to claim ownership of the process. While there remains much work to be done before the prototyping methods available to them allow the same level of flexibility and suitability as the techniques for traditional products, there are already sufficient tools, techniques and knowledge available to enable a more prototype-centric approach than typically occurs.

Universities need to embrace and teach these available techniques and develop new ones. Only by stretching designers' prototyping technique toolbox will users start to experience a greater range of fully integrated and innovative computer-embedded products.

NOTE

1. The Programme for Advanced Interactive Prototype Research, www.paipr.wordpress .com.

FURTHER READING

Buchenau, M., and Suri, J. F. (2000), 'Experience Prototyping', in *Proceedings of the Conference on Designing Interactive Systems: Processes, Practices, Methods, and Techniques*, New York: ACM, 424–33.

Burleson, W., Jenson, C. N., Raaschou, T., and Frohold, S. (2007), 'Sprock-it: A Physically Interactive Play System', *IDC '07. Proceedings of the 6th International Conference on Interaction Design and Children, Aalborg, Denmark*, New York: ACM, 125–8.

Buxton, W. (2001), 'Less is More (More or Less)', in P. Denning (ed.), *The Invisible Future: The Seamless Integration of Technology in Everyday Life*, New York: McGraw Hill.

Buxton, W. (2007), 'Sketching User Experiences: Getting the Design Right and the Right Design', San Francisco: Morgan Kaufmann.

Cooper, A. (2004), *The Inmates Are Running the Asylum: Why High Tech Products Drive Us Crazy and How to Restore the Sanity*, Indianapolis, IN: Sams.

Culverhouse, I. (2012), 'Investigation into the Potential of a Novel Rapid Low Fidelity Interactive Prototyping Technique for the Design development of Computer Embedded Devices', PhD thesis, University of Wales, UK.

Culverhouse, I., and Gill, S. (2009), 'Bringing Concepts to Life: Introducing a Rapid Interactive Sketch Modelling Toolkit for Industrial Designers', in *Proceedings of the 3rd International Conference on Tangible and Embedded Interaction*, New York: ACM, 363–6.

Gill, S. (2003), 'Developing Information Appliance Design Tools for Designers', *Personal and Ubiquitous Computing*, 7/3–4: 159–62.

Gill, S. (2009), 'Six Challenges Facing User-Orientated Industrial Design', *Design Journal*, 12/1: 41–67.

Gill, S., Loudon, G., and Walker, D. (2008), 'Designing a Design Tool: Working with Industry to Create an Information Appliance Design Methodology', *Journal of Design Research (JDR)*, 7/2: 97–119. doi: 10.1504/JDR.2008.020851.

Gill, S., Walker, D., Loudon, G., Dix, A., Woolley, A., Ramduny-Ellis, D., and Hare, J. (2008), 'Rapid Development of Tangible Interactive Appliances: Achieving the Fidelity/Time Balance', in E. Hornecker, A. Schmidt and B. Ullmer (eds), Special Issue on Tangible and Embedded Interaction, *International Journal of Arts and Technology*, 1/3–4: 309–31.

Greenberg, S., and Fitchett, C. (2001), 'Phidgets: Easy Development of Physical Interfaces through Physical Widgets', in *Proceedings of the 14th Annual ACM Symposium on User Interface Software and Technology*, New York: ACM, 209–18.

Hare, J., Gill, S., Loudon, G., Ramduny-Ellis, D., and Dix, A. (2009), 'Physical Fidelity: Exploring the Importance of Physicality on Physical-Digital Conceptual Prototyping', *Human-Computer Interaction—INTERACT 2009, Lecture Notes in Computer Science*, vol. 5726, Uppsala, Sweden: Springer, 217–30.

Hartmann, B., Abdulla, L., Klemmer, S., and Mittal, M. (2007), 'Authoring Sensor-based Interactions by Demonstration with Direct Manipulation and Pattern Recognition', in *Proceedings of ACM CHI 2007 Conference on Human Factors in Computing Systems*, New York: ACM, 145–54.

Hollan, J., Hutchins, E., and Kirsh, D. (2000), 'Distributed Cognition: Toward a New Foundation for Human-Computer Interaction Research', *ACM Transactions on Computer-Human Interaction*, 7/2: 174–96.

Loudon, G. (2006), 'Nice Technology, Shame about the Product', *Communications Engineer*, 4/4: 12–15.

Maulsby, D., Greenberg, S., and Mander, R. (1993), 'Prototyping an Intelligent Agent through Wizard of Oz', in *ACM SIGCHI Conference on Human Factors in Computing Systems*, Amsterdam: ACM, 277–84.

McGurk, H., and McDonald, J. (1978), 'Visual Influences on Speech Perception Processes', *Perception & Psychophysics*, 24/3: 253–7.

Nam, T. J., and Woohan, L. (2003), 'Integrating Hardware and Software: Augmented Reality Based Prototyping Method for Digital Products', in *Proceedings of CHI 2003 Conference on Human Factors in Computing Systems*, New York: ACM, 956–7.

Norman, D. A. (1988), *The Psychology of Everyday Things*, New York: Basic Books.

Schrage, M. (1999), *Serious Play: How the World's Best Companies Simulate to Innovate*, Cambridge, MA: Harvard Business School Press.

Sharp, J. A., Wright, D., Sharp, D., and Petzny, C. (1996), 'The Virtual Simulation of a Product: A Comparison with Reality', in *Proceedings of the first Asia Pacific Conference on Computer Human Interaction, APCHI'96, Singapore*, Singapore: Information Technology Institute, 279–84.

Snyder, C. (2003), *Paper Prototyping*, San Francisco: Morgan Kaufmann.

Thomas, T. J., Meech, J. F., and Macredie, R. D. (1995), 'A Framework for the Development of Information Appliances', *ACM SIGICE Bulletin*, 21/1: 15–19.

Villar, N., and Gellerson, H. (2007), 'A Malleable Control Structure for Softwired User Interfaces', in *Proceedings of Tangible and Embedded Interaction Conference (TEI '07)*, New York: ACM, 49–56.

11 THE RIP+MIX METHOD AND REFLECTION ON ITS PROTOTYPES

ROSAN CHOW

INTRODUCTION

Since 2007 I have been arguing for and developing a design approach called Case Transfer and a design method called RIP+MIX. Although serious undertakings have been given to these activities, I have rather intuitively claimed that my research process is akin to prototyping. To assess the assertion, this chapter explores my research process in the context of prototyping. It is divided into two parts: in the first section, discourse concentrates on the assumptions, theories and research results of Case Transfer and RIP+MIX, and it draws some implications for craft research and practice. In the second section, discussion attends to the opportunity to reflect on the process of developing the projective or forecasting method RIP+MIX and to link it to the theme of prototyping. Here, the discourse concentrates on raising issues rather than reporting the knowledge gained due to the embryonic stage of the work in this context. To be clear, what I will describe is retrospective, a kind of postrationalization and constructive account.

CASE TRANSFER

Case Transfer is based on two assumptions.[1] Firstly, projecting new artefacts is independent from analysing and understanding design context, including user needs and wants. Secondly, existing artefacts are knowledge sources for projection of the new. Currently, the received view is that the design process begins with rapid ethnographic study of users and use contexts. Study results then form the basis or design requirements by which designers might create innovative products or services. In brief, design follows user study. Underlying this view is the belief that in order to design, the design context or the design problem must first be understood. However, this view is conditionally useful but not always appropriate for all design situations. As argued by Jonas (2007) and Nelson and Stolterman (2003), understanding design problems does not guarantee generating design solutions. The competence to analyse design context is different and independent from, though intimately related to, the competence to make design proposals. It is not (logically) necessary, but only conditional for the design process to begin with analysis followed by projection. Not only is it not logically necessary, but it is at times even advantageous to begin a design project with imagining design alternatives. Here, it is suggested that the more undetermined the design situation, the more suitable it is to begin the design process with projection (Chow and Jonas 2010). This claim is supported by the fact that context is flexible and subject to change by design or, more precisely, by the interaction between people and artefacts. New design artefacts facilitate new contexts, new users, new needs and new wants. In other words, when there is no definite problem or identified context, as in the so-called exploratory projects, the focus should be on envisioning new designs.

Another assumption underlying the mantra that design follows user study is that users know what they want and like, and their knowledge can be beneficial to designing. Without contradicting this, design artefacts also embody knowledge that is beneficial to designing. In this discourse, design is taken to be a historical discipline, and the design knowledge base to be the artefacts. Designed artefacts (can) serve as an archive or a construction kit allowing reconfiguration. We take as fact that artefacts embody knowledge, as the specific practice of reverse-engineering to the whole field of archaeology is operated upon this belief. My interest in artefacts is not so much about understanding the past as about looking into the future. I hypothesize that existing designed artefacts are knowledge sources for projection and that we can take knowledge from one artefact and put it in another domain or context to create something new. This taking is what I call Transfer, and there are three types of transfer specified—namely, Local, Regional and Long-Distance. In Local Transfer, knowledge is taken within the same domain; in Regional, across similar domains; and in Long-Distance, across different domains. These three transfers have been explored in a series of quasi-experiments to construct a conceptual framework for further method development. In the first study, two designers collected and analysed mobile phones (Local), mobile objects (Regional) and avant-garde objects (Long-Distance) and used them to conceive new mobile communication devices. The same study was repeated by six groups of design students from two different universities. In the second study, two design students collected and analysed mobile internet services (Local), noninternet-based services (Regional) and performing art practices (Long-Distance) and used these to conceive new mobile internet services. The basic techniques of Grounded Theory were followed to observe and analyse the research results. Comparative coding, making memos, conceptual-izing and concurrent literature review were performed as the core concepts were constructed. These studies showed consistently that transfer was productive al-though piecemeal. Both formal and contextual elements of the designed artefacts were transferable, including physical and sensual form, material, function and feature, character, and context of use. Regional Transfer was the most productive.

ARTEFACTS ACT AS SIGNS

As the studies were being carried out and observations were made of the results, I turned to Peirce's abduction and semiotic (Chow 2009; Chow, Jonas and Schaeffer 2009). I appealed to Peirce because of existing research on applying abduction to explain analogy making (McJohn 1993; Sowa 2006; Sowa and Majumdar 2003) as well as previous arguments raised in design (March 1984; Roozenburg 1993). I accept transfer as abductive reasoning, and abduction as a semiotic process. The Peircean system of signs is not only a classification scheme but also describes how people reason and make inferences about the world. Peircean signs are forms of abduction, induction and deduction (Chow 2009). I see transfer as abductive-reasoning, and there is a sign relation between source (existing products and services) and the target (new concepts). During transfer, the sources act as signs, the new concepts are objects of signs and the designers perceive the sources as de-noting the objects. The results have been interpreted from the quasi-experiments; in terms of these signs, see Table 11.1.

Table 11.1   Designerly interpretation of six Peircean open signs/abductions.

Open	Icon	Index	Symbol
Tone	Hunch *(Feeling of possibility)*		
Token	Form *(Individual function or feature, material, physical/sensual form)*	Context *(Stakeholders, purpose, needs, wants, context of use, manufacturing process)*	
Type	Metaphor *(Relation between function, material and form)*	Scenario *(Network, culture)*	Principle

Hunch: a feeling that an object or a service might have some possibility of being transferred.

Form: an individual physical shape, material, function or feature. *The designer took an organic shape of a shell to give form to a product.*

Metaphor: some relation of individual design elements. *The designer took the model of the public bus system as a metaphor for a public phone service.*

Context: an object or service pointing to individual cause or consequence, such as stakeholder needs, manufacturing processes or anything that has an impact on how the object comes to be. *The designer interpreted a pistol as pointing to a dangerous situation. The designer thought of a rescue call feature on a mobile phone for that situation.* This sign is believed to be very important, as it has led to several interesting concepts in the quasi-experiments.

Scenario: a product and service pointing to some relation, such as a network of people or culture. In the quasi-experiments, there was no Scenario found, and this deserves further investigation.

Principle: a product or service is interpreted as referring to some rules by virtue of a disposition or a habit. *The designer associated a pistol with a mobile communication device as a result of a disposition or habit.*

It was also discovered that Local Transfer is not very productive because the results resemble the sources so much so that they can be considered copies. Regional and Long-Distance Transfers tend to generate novel and more interesting results. This observation is in line with the general belief in the creative power of employing metaphor and analogy. However, it was also noticed that transfer is easier in Regional Transfer than in Long-Distance Transfer. Arguably, it is easier to see resemblance between similar things, as in Regional Transfer, than different things, as in Long-Distance Transfer.

It is proffered that the principles and methods underlying Case Transfer be applicable to Craft as much as to Design. An analogy between the two practices can easily be made. The adapted Peircean system of signs is a useful tool to analyse or interpret how a craft object embodies knowledge. An experienced craft person arguably uses this system of signs intuitively; however, the formal nature of the system allows explicit discussion and communication that is helpful for craft research. Artefacts embody knowledge because they act as signs. Artefacts can point us to their formal, material, efficient and final causes. We give the name Form to the first two causes and the name Context to the latter two causes. Formal relation is named Metaphor, and Contextual relation is named Scenario. The habit or tendency to interpret artefacts in such a way is named Principle. At this point, it is important to make a qualification: artefacts *cannot* speak for themselves. As signs, artefacts need to be interpreted in order for the embodied knowledge to have meaning for us as individuals.

RIP+MIX

With understanding derived from previous research, Case Transfer was tested in a real-life project together with the design school at the University of Dundee in 2009. The design task was to imagine information and communication products and services (ICPS) for elderly people. The research question was 'How effective is Case Transfer in projecting these new designs?' The primary intention was to test a method under development rather than observe and inquire into a natural phenomenon. This is an important delineation. The project was a form of prototype-testing. The team was using Case Transfer (as a prototype) for a specific design project; their experiences and feedback formed the basis for reflection and refinement of Case Transfer. The study suggests Case Transfer has the following advantages and characteristics:

1. It provides a method of making design knowledge visible and usable.
2. Highly productive in terms of generating ideas.
3. Counterpoints and complements User-Centred Design.
4. Offers scope for the involvement of nondesigners—because the initial stages do not assume prior design knowledge.
5. Takes design away from the computer, emphasizing physical recording, sketching and collaborative working.

From the study results, a method named RIP+MIX has been devised: a six-step process with a specific question aligned to each stage is proposed. See Figure 11.1.

Step 1   What products and services exist?
         Collect existing targeted artefacts as a *baseline*.

Step 2   What are similar?
         Collect similar artefacts as *sources* for transfer.

Step 3   What are the forms and contexts of the sources?
         Analyse (rip) sources in design terms and create *signs*.

Step 4   What can be mixed?
         Transfer (mix) 'signs' to create new *concepts*.

Step 5   How good are the concepts?
         Evaluate and develop concepts with users to generate *facts*.

Step 6   What should be made?
         Finalize concepts with stakeholders to generate *results*.

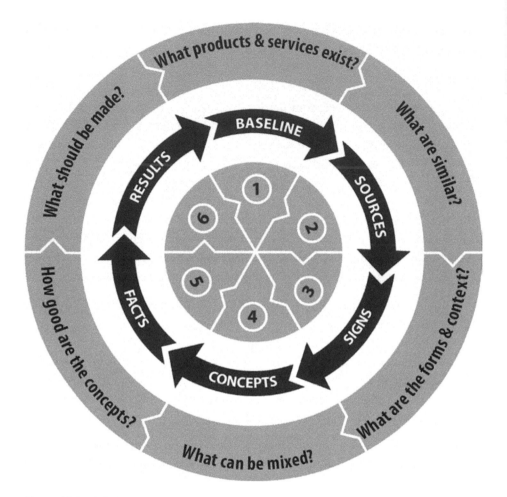

Figure 11.1 RIP+MIX process.

RIP+MIX 2.0

Despite the research results and experiences, the effects of sources on transfer or the steps 5 and 6 are not yet fully understood. To make RIP+MIX more robust, the following research questions are currently being investigated:

1. What are the criteria to determine, collect and represent sources?
2. What are the criteria for choosing concepts generated from RIP+MIX?
3. What are the roles of end users and other stakeholders for evaluating and choosing concepts? What processes and methods can be employed?

As part of the investigation, the process has been refined and a new version developed, RIP+MIX 2.0, with the following steps (see Figure 11.2):

1. Decide project type and approach (new).
2. Identify sources (new).
3. Collect and represent sources (previous step 1 Baseline and step 2 Sources).
4. RIP+MIX signs (previous step 3 Signs and step 4 Concepts).
5. Sort, choose and develop concepts (previous step 5 Facts).
6. Evaluate use cases (previous step 6 Results).

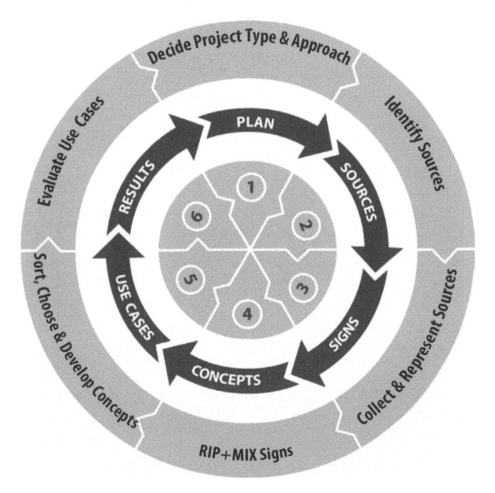

Figure 11.2   RIP+MIX 2.0 process.

Table 11.2   The Determinacy Guide: Design situation, indeterminacy and appropriate approach.

	Function (Technology)	Form (Design)	Context (User)	Goal (Needs & Wants)	Type of Project	Suitable Process	Suitable Approach
1	X	X	X	X	No project	APS	Problem solving
2	X	X	X		Repurpose		
3	X	X		X	Marketing		
4		X	X	X	Re-engineering		
5	X		X	X	Redesign		
6			X	X	Market-driven		
7	X		X		Design Ethnography		
8		X	X		Unlikely		
9	X	X			Cultural Probe		
10	X			X	Innovative Design		
11		X		X	Fiction-driven		
12			X		New Market		
13		X			Unusual		
14	X				Technological Push		
15				X	Open	PAS	Case Transfer
16					Just for Fun		

X   = determined, known, certain

     = highly undetermined projects

     = fairly undetermined projects

APS   = Analysis, Projection, Synthesis [a]
PAS   = Projection, Analysis, Synthesis

[a] Analysis, Projection and Synthesis are concepts Wolfgang Jonas uses to describe
the domains of knowing in design. The APS and PAS describe the possible sequences of design projects.

Tools are also being developed to support each step and to test the process and tools in a real-life project. At the time of writing, a new step has been added as the first step of RIP+MIX 2.0—namely, 'Decide project type and approach'. For this step, we have also developed a guide (tentatively called the Determinacy Guide), see Table 11.2. The Determinacy Guide characterizes different types of projects and indicates their relationship to Case Transfer. This new step and new tool are important as they provide the basis for the subsequent step to identify sources systematically. To make the step and the guide operational, four elements or variables—namely, Function (technology), Form (design), Context (user) and Goal (needs and wants) were introduced to describe a design situation. The assumption made was that given any design project, one or more of these elements are undetermined, unknown and uncertain. The higher the number of undetermined variables, the more undetermined the design situation and the more suitable the Case Transfer approach. Furthermore, Case Transfer is especially suitable when the Goal is unknown as the strength of Case Transfer is to create or identify new Goals by means of projecting artefacts. It was identified that the real-life project in which we are testing RIP+MIX 2.0 is a Technological Push project, and Case Transfer is an appropriate approach.

In a Technological Push project, the only known variable is the technical function, in this case, an advanced display technology. The known variable is that by which to identify Local, Regional and Long-Distance sources. From this variable, artefacts that have a function that is the same as, similar to and different from the display function can be identified. Examples of Local sources are magazines, posters, signs, watches, e-books, iPads, notebook and e-paper. Regional source examples are smoke, steam, toaster, cup, hearing aid and microphone. Long-Distance sources are state-of-the-art and craft objects. RIP+MIX 2.0 continues to be tested and developed, as are further tools. For example, we must match the Determinacy Guide with the adapted Peircean system of signs. Furthermore, it is also expected that new goals that RIP+MIX can achieve will be discovered. In short, we are still prototyping.

REFLECTING ON THE PROTOTYPES OF RIP+MIX

In the process of design and craft, prototypes are indispensable. Donald Schön (1984) and his subscribers teach us that sketches (which I consider a form of prototype) 'talk back' to us. Sketches and prototypes are not only the results of designing but they are also tools for (further) designing. With this understanding of prototypes, I will reflect on the process of prototyping the RIP+MIX method. First I will view prototyping through psychological research on 'concept'.

For a long time perception has been considered to be separate from and subordinated to conception. However, the thesis of an embodied mind suggests otherwise. Concepts are tethered to perception and action, and mind is grounded in experiences. We have minds and form concepts because we need to function in and deal with a changing environment in which we are a part. Mind is adaptive and flexible. Concepts are not fixed but rather created on the fly in particular situations (Gabora, Rosch and Aerts 2008). Conceptualizing is context sensitive or embodied. This perspective on perception and conception (or body and mind) is personally helpful for understanding this specific prototyping process.

Prototypes are not a representation of concepts already generated by the mind, but rather they contribute to creating new design or craft concepts. I would like to entertain that prototypes are critical because they allow perceptual experiences. These experiences change the context in which and by which we conceive new designs and craft objects. This proposition is related to Peirce's view on Abduction as fundamentally perceptual but is also supported by the groundbreaking Prototype Theory by the psychologist Eleanor Rosch (1978). According to Rosch, when people categorize, they match it to a Prototype that has the most salient features of the category.[2] A swallow, not a penguin, is a Prototype of the category bird. Besides, according to Rosch, Prototype is a Basic Level of categorization. Chair is a Basic Level concept, while furniture is a Superordinate, and a kitchen chair is a Subordinate. Unlike Superordinate concepts, Basic Level concepts are perceivable and full of informational and often imagistic content. This informational content is less specific, however, than that of the Subordinate concepts. Basic Level concepts are very important because conceptualizing tends to use these as a base. In other words, Basic Level concepts help us think in more detail or more abstractly. I suggest that Design and Craft prototypes, being perceptual, function as a Basic Level concept that helps us to think more abstractly and in more detail. Prototyping is interplay between perceiving and conceiving. When I recall the process I have gone through to develop RIP+MIX, I see myself prototyping in the sense that I describe here.

When I first developed the Case Transfer approach, I had in mind a three-step method: (a) Collect, (b) Analyse and (c) Transfer. This can be considered the first prototype which became the RIP+MIX method. The first prototype is based on the assumptions and theoretical orientation that are described above. To make the first prototype, a designer and a design student were invited to collect, analyse and transfer intuitively. As with designers and craft persons imagining something new/uncertain, the intention then was to try it and to see what might happen. I observed, recorded and thought/fought over the first prototype. In retrospect, without the first prototype, I would not have identified patterns that demanded explanation and would not have turned to Peirce. By logic or happy coincidence or both, his system of signs seemed to be helpful to describe and explain the transfer process and results. In essence, the adapted Peircean system of signs would not have emerged without the help of the first prototype. Although Peirce helped me to explain transfer and to develop a system for interpretation and investigation, of equal importance, the first prototype supported understanding and identification of some new uses of his theories. I had previously taken an interest in Peircean abduction but had never been able to operationalize it for design. The first prototype, being on the Basic Level and thus being perceivable, has helped me understand the very abstract concept of abduction, which was otherwise impossible. It helps to remember that we create concepts on the fly and in context; by implication, the first prototype has created a new context to interplay with Peirce and has facilitated new insights and understanding to emerge. The juxtaposition between the Peircean system of signs and the sketches generated by transferring has resulted in a framework, as described above. I have begun to use the framework to analyse and transfer knowledge embodied in artefacts. Although its values have yet to be fully tested, the framework has enabled further development of RIP+MIX and RIP+MIX 2.0. The interplay of perceiving and conceiving was indeed present throughout the process of prototyping RIP+MIX. If what I am speculating has value, then I must draw some implications for design and craft research.

Design is often presented as a way of knowing—a way of knowing the problem and a way of knowing the solution (Cross 2006). I am speculating here that prototyping, being indispensable in design and craft, is a way of knowing the abstract in a way not possible without it. This knowing is, of course, not making claims about truth corresponding with observable phenomena. This knowing is more about realizing the potential of a knowledge claim. Like all followers of Pragmatism, I believe that knowledge without consequence is not knowledge at all. We take for granted that abstract theory or knowledge constructed in different analytical disciplines is applied in design. One might say I apply Peircean semiotic for RIP+MIX as if it is automatic and not mediated. However, to apply theory, we need a mediator, and the scientists call this mediation operationalization. Operationalization is the 'development of specific research procedures (operations) that will result in empirical observations representing those concepts in the real world' (Babbie 2010: 140). Prototypes seem to be such mediators. The implication drawn from this speculation is that besides being a practical tool to understand design problems and create solutions, prototype can also be a research tool to understand the potential of the abstract. The final product of design is also a prototype, a mediator for further conceptualization and knowing.

This is in line with the thinking underlying RIP+MIX, which sees artefacts as knowledge sources for projection.

CLOSING REMARK

The development of the method RIP+MIX has been reported, and reflection on the process of this development has been offered. As outlined in the introduction, the latter is more about raising issues of interest than reporting knowledge gained. If any international peers have the same issues and/or if colleagues have articulated them, I welcome any comments and insights you may wish to share. These can contribute to the continually evolving articulation of the value and use(s) of prototyping in design.

NOTES

1. This text on assumptions of Case Transfer is a summary of the arguments elaborated in Chow and Jonas 2010.
2. When the word 'Prototype' is capitalized, it refers to Rosch's concept.

FURTHER READING

Babbie, E. (2010), *The Practice of Social Research*, Belmont: Wadsworth.

Chow, R. (2005), *For User Study. The Implication of Design*, PhD thesis, Design, University of Arts Braunschweig, Germany.

Chow, R. (2009), 'Abduction Revisited', in J. Verbeke and A. Jakimowicz (eds), *Communicating by Design*, Brussels: Chalmers University of Technology & Hogeschool voor Wetenschap & Kunst, 193–7.

Chow, R., and Jonas, W. (2010), 'Case Transfer: A Design Approach by Artefacts and Projection', *Design Issues*, 26: 9–19.

Chow, R, Jonas, W., and Schaeffer, N. (2009), 'Peircean Abduction, Signs & Design Transfer', in J. Malins (ed.), *8th European Academy of Design Conference 'Design Connexity'*, Aberdeen: Robert Gordon University, 87–91.

Cross, N. (2006), *Designerly Way of Knowing*, London: Springer-Verlag.

Gabora, L., Rosch, E., and Aerts, D. (2008), 'Toward an Ecological Theory of Concepts', *Ecological Psychology*, 20: 84–116.

Jonas, W. (2007), 'Research through DESIGN through Research—A Cybernetic Model of Designing Design Foundation', *Kybernetes*, 36: 1362–80.

March, L. (1984), 'The Logic of Design', in N. Cross (ed.), *Developments in Design Methodology*, Chichester: John Wiley & Sons, 265–76.

McJohn, S.M. (1993), 'On Uberty: Legal Reasoning by Analogy and Peirce's Theory of Abduction', *Willamette Law Review*, 29: 191–235.

Nelson, H., and Stolterman, E. (2003), *The Design Way: The Intentional Change in an Unpredictable World*, Englewood Cliffs, NJ: Educational Technology.

Roozenburg, N.F.M. (1993), 'On the Pattern of Reasoning in Innovative Design', *Design Studies*, 14: 4–18.

Rosch, E. (1978), 'Principles of Categorization', in E. Rosch and B. Lloyd (eds), *Cognition and Categorization*, Hillsdale, NJ: Lawrence Erlbaum.

Schön, D. (1984), *The Reflective Practitioner: How Professionals Think in Action*, New York: Basic Books.

Sowa, J. (2006), 'Peirce's Contributions to the 21st Century', in H. Schärfe, P. Hitzler and P. Øhrstrøm (eds), *Conceptual Structures: Inspiration and Application. 14th International Conference on Conceptual Structures, ICCS 2006, Lecture Notes in Artificial Intelligence 4068*, Aalborg, Denmark: Springer, 54–69.

Sowa, J. F., and Majumdar, A. K. (2003), 'Analogical Reasoning', in A. Aldo, W. Lex and B. Ganter (eds), *International Conference on Conceptual Structures, Volume 2747, Conceptual Structures for Knowledge Creation and Communication, Lecture Notes in Artificial Intelligence*, Dresden, Germany: Springer-Verlag, 16–36.

CLOSING REMARK

LOUISE VALENTINE

Design and craft are activities requiring freedom—freedom to explore, to allow imagination and creativity to range widely and to bring knowledge and expertise alive in a wild, uninhibited dance. The activity is a dialogue following a nonlinear path from conception of ideas to final real-world product (in all its myriad of form). Whilst it appears to contrast with conventional linear formulation, it remains a process of systematic, implicit reasoning using planned and unplanned iterations, feedback and feed-forward loops, albeit in an apparently chaotic way. The process involves looking, listening and questioning, allowing collective thoughts to levitate—to sit suspended in the mind and be given space, through time, to develop as the processes of problem identification and problem-solving unfold. This suspension of thought allows a pattern to evolve, providing an individual with a picture, which depicts the interrelationship(s) between different and often contrasting elements of a situation. It is visual-thinking and inherently demands a close working relation with intuition (Valentine 2004). This human-centred perspective on the process of making coupled with an inquiry into cultivating the capabilities and capacities of designers underpins *Prototype*.

In today's world where there is an inordinately high pace of change, the boundaries between subjects are increasingly blurry, and their relationships are increasingly complex. The central challenge irrespective of profession is the interdependent and interrelated nature of problems. Here, transcendence and transformation are central themes. Here, the resultant space is highly dynamic with an elevated demand for the effective exchange of knowledge and skills across cultures and languages—an environment that stresses a rethink of how we think and why we think the way we do. In these new circumstances, there is a growing need to work together in an intentional manner to resolve the increasingly complex problems, sharing insights gathered from a rich range of perspectives to dissolve the assumptions hindering progress. High levels of uncertainty are the norm in these extreme situations.

The complex problems we confront are a consequence of our past thinking and actions. In order to resolve these new, unique situations, Einstein (cited in Calaprice 2005) suggests we need to change our mindsets from the ones that created the problems in the first place. The chaotic phase calls for a lessening of the need to emphasize difference and a heightening of our understanding of similarities and relevance between subjects. Key to moving forward in this interconnected framework is sagacious engagement, so that awareness of its implications can be achieved and mindfully applied.

Of particular interest from this emergent landscape is the impact change has on the practice of making design and craft because an individual's experiential and subjective perspective is integral to the process of conceiving and planning. The new environment changes our mindset, alters the values underpinning the creative act of making, and with it, transforms the notion of basic terms, such as 'design process' and 'craft practice'. New ways of working (process) are as important as making new work (product).

British designer Anthony Dunne exemplifies the way in which designers explore alternative approaches to practice, and his genotype models concentrate on cultivating the germ of an idea. The genotype 'deflects attention from an aesthetics of construction to an aesthetics of use. It depends on the view that a design idea can transcend its material and structural reality and function critically, in relation to social systems, for example, rather than visual culture' (Dunne 2005: 91). Drawing on the work of Michele De Lucchi (1979, cited in Dunne 2005), Dunne exemplifies the value of the genotype and the alternative model that it offers, noting, '[t]hey offer real experiences of ideas rather than unreal experiences of unrealized products, and accept that these ideas will be consumed through books and exhibition not in the marketplace' (92). In *Hertzian Tales*, Dunne describes conceptual design proposals for 'post-optimal electronic objects' (i.e. objects intended to raise questions and provoke discussion rather than be mass produced). For example, 'Electroclimates' is a pillow with an integrated LCD screen that makes visible the patterns of electroclimatic changes from telephones, garage door openers, and so on. Inspired by devices such as barometers that expose the unseen aspects of space, 'it would be an aid for poetically inhabiting the electrosphere, a contemplative object revealing the hertzian nature of our environment' (Dunne 2005: 124). 'Tunable Cities' uses radio waves to explore spaces and attempts to shift the view of radio as energy towards something more tangible, an indicator of the surroundings. The proposed object, a car radio, picked up sounds from illegal bugging devices, baby monitors and radio-tagged birds and explored areas where the sounds transmitted were directly influenced by the cars in the area. All of these objects are examples of the genotype, containing only the best possible physical description of the idea, with little concern for usability. These 'Sublime Gadgets' (Dunne 2005) do not initially appear to be related to prototyping, as Dunne states, 'the proposals are not intended for mass production or even prototyping' (2005: 123). However, each proposal describes the transition from embryonic concept to genotype and how the physical and conceptual develop side by side.

Building on Anthony Dunne's concept of the genotype, Hazel White's work explores the use of objects as interaction devices in digital media where clarification and progression of the gene of an idea is the focus of activity rather than the production of a fully resolved object. Drawing on her background in jewellery design with a craft ethos, White wrestles with a variety of questions: can jewellery be an intimate physical reminder to interact with other people, the self or life in general? In today's world, where we are always 'switched-on' to work and the act of 'consuming' information, could craft act as a physical prompt to 'switch off' and concentrate on the personal, a more spiritual perspective of life? In *Hamefarer's Kist*, White uses a crafted cultural artefact to explore meaning and aesthetics in computing, testing handmade knitted textiles as a tangible interface to gather, preserve and share personal memories. *Hamefarer's Kist* is mindfully designed to support geographically remote communities and geographically distant family members to care for one another. Through the discussion in this book, White is perceived to advocate for technologically led design to have deeper meaning in people's lives, where people of every age can find relevance and genuine conversations with new technologies. Her work explores the use of objects as interaction devices, where clarification and progression of the gene of an idea is the focus of activity. In doing so, she indirectly posits the genotype as a means of raising the level of innovation within one's creative portfolio. This act of increasing innovation is the priority rather than the notion of creating a fully resolved and unique handmade object.

Leonardo Bonanni, Amanda Parkes and Hiroshi Ishii's notion of 'Future Craft' (2008) discusses the transformative nature of interaction through digital media and how it has impacted product design specifically: 'a design methodology which applies emerging digital tools and processes to product design toward new objects that are socially and environmentally sustainable' (1). The term 'Future Craft' refers to the graduate curriculum at MIT, in Cambridge, Massachusetts, (which Bonanni and his colleagues deliver) that 'considers how the processes of design and production can be used to reflect new social values and to change dominant cultural practices'. The educational agenda is driven by global issues, such as healthcare, poverty, ethics and sustainability, and is explored from three perspectives—namely, Local Design, Public Design and Personal Design. The work signifies and evidences the shift away from the materiality of craft, removing it as a concern with beauty, material and techniques. These remain important tenets, but what is of central importance is the scenario in which emerging problems and methodologies are experimented with and explored. It also highlights the importance of the term and ethos of communities (be they virtual or real) and the relation between local and global in our action-based world.

Visual artist and computer scientist John Maeda (2006; see also Maeda and Bermont 2011) offers the 'prototype-a-thon', a way of working which invites mass prototyping on a single theme as a way to prompt innovation over a sustained and intense period of time. Working at the interface between art, design and technology, Maeda's work explores the development of new technologies to help improve and simplify the lives of everyday people. While many interesting ideas can be generated, the prototyping approach itself is an invaluable creative tool for rapid brainstorming and problem-solving. A sandpit is an example from British academe, whereby dynamic research-led teams are formed to offer multispecialist perspectives that have the relevant knowledge to evolve radical solutions. They are similar in nature to the 'prototype-a-thon', 'hackathon', and 'make-a-thon' (by IDEO), which are also intensive, interactive and collaborative endeavours (originated within software development but now extend beyond this) and are examples of contemporary approaches to the concept of prototyping. These examples are by no means exhaustive and are used to highlight the changes witnessed in prototyping.

Beyond the conceptual approaches to prototyping is a new aesthetic within creative practice arising from the hybrid and digital forms of, and concepts for, creative practice. Hybridization of disciplines, ideas or methods has presented a means to resist and experiment with traditional boundaries and perceptions of the self (as maker) and design and craft (as knowledge, meaning and form). According to Jorunn Veiteberg (drawing on the work of Homi K. Bhabha), 'this intellectual arena or "Third Space" annuls the perceptions of history which constitutes it, and new structures continuously arise instead. But, of course, the new will be full of traces and impressions of the feelings and practices that have permeated the process. Thus, in the third space, ambiguous practices will be those that are typical, and it is possible for different practices to live side by side—without hierarchic ranking—simultaneously' (Veiteberg 2005: 39).

The 'third space' is design and craft as an intellectual activity attending to complex situations and environments, where the multifaceted, multifunctional and formational act of making things is retained as a central component. Virtualization and the associated digital tools is another notable facilitator of change within creative practice during the 1990s and early twenty-first century. It is a key tenet of many hybrid practices and concept(s). Designer and MIT professor Neri Oxman's organic architecture based on biomimicry and computation exposes hybridity and the nature of postdisciplinary practice and in doing so exemplifies the shift in emphasis in prototyping, moving it from being considered with form and function to an activity concerned with performance and behaviour. Similarly, in a conceptual sense and from a practical perspective, the international collaborative practice of Alex Murray-Leslie, Melissa Logan and Kiki Moorse (who merge performance, art, avant-pop, electronica, fashion, politics and consumerism) through their 'Chicks on Speed' project is a pertinent example of modern prototyping in the creative arts. Chicks on Speed (2010) is an ever-changing multidisciplinary art group who apply punk-inspired DIY ethics to interrogate the boundaries of art, craft, fashion and music. Their collaborative approach and radically experimental creative practice offers an alternative viewpoint and physical manifestation for appreciating the concept of hybridization. The British product artist Geoffrey Mann's work also involves a mashing of subjects. His work cuts across the areas of film, sculpture, physics, craft and design (http://www.mrmann.co.uk). The visual methodology he nurtures is one that is not solely art, craft or product design but a combination of all three, each given varying degrees of attention within a project and across his portfolio. His work is concerned with the sinuous passage of time and space and is to date primarily materially manifest in glass and ceramics through the latest advancements in technology. One aspect of his work is to assess the notion of touching motion; an intangible concept in that no one knows how motion feels (despite it being part of our everyday lives). He does this by prototyping in different cultures, environments, materials, sizes and technology. Mann uses prototyping as a way of facilitating knowledge, understanding and executing the abstract. He probes the issue of motion, and in doing so, he offers a visual and social commentary on how to question and respond to a basic premise of the human condition. In this sense, design and craft is an intellectual experiment—a process concerned with uniting a range of different creative endeavours, a space in-between established fields of enquiry and an aesthetic commentary.

This burst of new thinking and increased attention to the act of prototyping in creative practice (in which an object is conceived) is of no surprise, for every prototype is orientated to the future—a means to an end beyond itself, a future in the present.

In this conceptual prototype, exposed in part in the form of a book, and through Michael Schrage's thoughts on 'the prototype as a hypothesis, the prototype as a marketplace and the prototype as a playground', a fundamentally different approach to how design and craft can rethink and work with the concept of prototyping is also suggested. In the context of creative visual practices, he offers a series of questions and interrelated themes with which to prod the effectiveness and value of one's ideas, be they individual and/or team-based acts. It facilitates a questioning of the values underpinning an individual's motivations to ascertain whether these values are essential to hindering progress. His theory of the craft of prototyping encourages the dynamic interaction of three design principles—hypothesis, marketplace and playground—in order to achieve a heightened level of innovation and impact, where craft is the 'enhancement of concept'. Inherent within his theory are four important details:

- Prototypes are as much cultural artefacts as technical objects. They reflect individual ingenuity as much as they embody institutional imperatives. Successful prototypes invite and encourage serious play. The prototype becomes as much a medium for interpersonal interaction as a tool for discovery, insight and test.
- The craft of prototyping transcends time and technology.
- Prototypes are media—places and platforms for collaborative creativity. They enable different ecologies and economics of innovative insight. They are a means to interpersonal—not just technical—ends.
- Prototypes frequently serve as lures and bait for creative contribution by others. The prototype becomes, in essence, an 'innovation invitation' for hypothesis, play and value exchange.

Schrage's chapter attends to the issues of creativity, reality, risk, rule-breaking and uncertainty. The central premise is that iterative prototyping can elevate a mediocre idea to greatness, and a 'great idea' is not an essential starting position. The overarching and most significant contribution Schrage's idea makes is that his proposition transcends discipline barriers. His approach (of charismatic prototyping as innovation-raising) is arguably as relevant to design and craft as it is to physics, to medical science, to sculpture.

The context and subject of change in design and design education is the focus of chapters by Fraser Bruce and Seaton Baxter, Rosan Chow, Steve Gill, Liz Sanders and Jan Pieter Stappers, albeit to lesser and greater degrees. Sanders's new Participatory Prototyping Cycle (PPC) model is similar to Schrage, in that it is concerned with innovation, but different in that it is less concerned with innovation raising than with innovation, appropriation. Sanders's short yet succinct overview of the evolutionary history of the prototype in design (from 1980 to 2010) presents the key attributes of the prototype's form and nature over the last thirty years—specifically, the migration from a fixation of designing objects to designing for people in the context of their lives. She captures the shifts from highly polished lifelike models to 'quick and dirty' snapshots of an idea, from prototypes for the final design development end to prototypes for the fuzzy front end of design, from prototypes for developing an understanding of the physical manifestation of a design to prototypes for creating new experiences, environments and methods. The clarity with which Sanders presents the changes and the emergence of change within design during 1980–2010, through the lens of prototyping, is itself a valuable contribution to our understanding of the shifting landscape of design and craft and the impact the emerging environments will have in the curricula for design and craft education. Her point of view on the culture of design and the prototyping process is a reminder that the use of design-thinking can be a gradual process and can address some of the more complex issues with which modern society is faced. Her PPC model expands the notion of prototyping from a physical construction to a convivial tool that has presence in both space and time and moves across the full design process as a 'generative seed'. Here, the form of the prototype can be a story and scenario as easily as it can be a speculative or representational object. The intent of the model is for sharing through collective making, telling and enacting. Her concept re-purposes prototyping, and her proposition is for educators to 'train designers on how to design and facilitate PPC appropriately', as she believes it offers a means with which to bridge the gap between design and research. As she says, 'The PPC is a model for cocreation in design. It invites relevant stakeholders into the design process and supplies them with tools, methods and activities that they can use without having education or experience as designers'. In upcoming design practices, Sanders believes the prototype will have a new ethos. It will have a greater concern for nurturing the collective exploration, expression and testing of hypotheses for 'future ways of living in the world' and be less concerned with offering a representation of a future object. The nature of the design process is also fundamentally challenged by Chow—specifically, the assumption that design should be led by observations made from studying people using design (existing or propositional) in the context of their lives. Her contribution to the experimental discourse is the collaborative and cultural process of testing a prototype on a local, national and international level: an alternative theory and method for working with the abstract in design. Chow champions the ability to imagine and to use the imagination more when dealing with indeterminate problems and uncertainty. Bruce and Baxter also promote greater use of the imagination as an alternative vista from which to consider developing design and design education, emphasizing the need to not only rely on what we know but also to be mindful of what we know about nature and its ecosystems. Learning to think through and about integrated and interrelated scenarios, which can take hundreds of years to create and thousands of years to evolve, is the essence of change in their proposition—inviting the 'maker' to fully consider an artificial design's 'ecosystem' and its natural design environment.

Sanders, Chow, and Bruce and Baxter inadvertently challenge the values underpinning design and craft, suggesting we rethink why and what we are planning and with whom and how we engage throughout the creative process. Indeed, they invite us to revisit our notion of 'the design process', suggesting that the traditional is redundant when dealing with modern complexities. The emphasis moves from design processes to multicultural human experiences, with concern for articulating why things need to happen rather than how and what does happen. Thereby, the new design practices question whether a design process is needed and critically assesses its impact, deciding whether it should occur or not.

The issue of manufacturing is never far from any discussion about design, craft and prototyping, and this volume is no different. Gill, Rossi and Stappers attend to the construction of prototypes in their respective stories about the making of specific examples of design and craft, in both historical and contemporary contexts. Rossi exposes an intimate relation and dedicated commitment between manufacturing and skilled artisans to deliver excellence in product design by discussing the relation between prototype and archetype. She draws attention to the central role prototypes play in the relationship between craft and design and exemplifies the prototype as a participant, facilitator, agitator and negotiator of change. In doing so, the values underpinning twentieth-century Italian design, such as partnership working, investment of quality time, sustained testing and development of ideas through model-making, are offered. Rossi argues that the mid-1960s marked a significant period of change in Italian design led by architects such as Andrea Branzi and designer Ettore Sottsass, shifting from prototyping towards open-ended exploration of ideas with highly conceptual and behavioural aims: from market driven to conceptually orientated design (an approach which can be connected or likened, in part, to UK designer Anthony Dunne's 1990s concept of the 'genotype', as his work also gives greater emphasis to concept and concept-testing without the need for full-scale production or mass-manufacturing considerations). Indeed, the Italian mid-twentieth-century design and craft production values arguably have much to offer the changing landscape of international design and craft and prototyping today. Nothing is truly without precedent, and history has much to teach us about how we manage ourselves now. Indeed, this is one example of the opportunity emerging from thematically driven transnational and interdisciplinary conversations in that it is possible to see connections between practices and learn about new ways of perceiving familiar subjects and/or perspectives. An increase in the visibility of sharing knowledge and experience arguably offers an opportunity to critically engage with our assumptions and achieve fresh insight. An assumption underpinning this book is that in order to intellectually progress design and craft, we must better understand the two in relation to each other and to disciplines outside of the traditional broad band. Another is that without an investment of time and the application of patience and respect, the pivotal yet silent act of trust cannot be achieved. The building of a shared language, which is an agreement of the values underpinning a joint venture, is subsequently in jeopardy. And if we are to sustain partnerships across and between knowledge domains in order to attend to the problems of our time, this activity and ability becomes core—indeed, it characterizes the design.

Stappers and Gill's conversations about the physical making of ideas offer insight and some empirical evidence of the importance of tangible prototypes in academic research and information appliance design. Stappers suggests that the rise in doctoral design programmes and graduates has brought about a significant change in education. Academic design research has given prototyping a new context within which to sit and with it, new meaning and form, which can be of value to design research, research in general and the building of new relations between academia and industry; prototypes are tools to explore phenomena as well as examples of a product or service under development. They are the means with which to confront theory and bridge the gap with practice by facilitating new and open-ended conversation. Gill's manufacturing tale is more technical in nature than Rossi and Stappers, yet his argument for better and quicker completion rates of tangible computer-embedded prototypes is as important an issue to include and consider in the emerging landscapes of design and craft. The production of 'things', especially computer-embedded things, will arguably continue at a relatively high rate, and resolving quality and cost issues will remain a consideration, especially for industrial product designers and manufacturers.

Stuart Brown deals directly with the act of sharing knowledge and expertise within the design of bespoke tools for pioneering surgeons, a process which denies the luxury of an indeterminate amount of time and space. His highly rhetorical approach to communicating the problem reveals a reality when seeking to achieve excellence in the service of medical science: perpetual questioning and partnership rather than collaboration. The rhetorical dimension is a way of adding meaning to the process and understanding of the subject to the team leader. Irrespective of an individual's knowledge of prototyping and/or keyhole surgery, Brown's discussion resonates. It offers insight into the relation between bespoke product design and surgery as well as clear explanation and description of prototyping in real-time worlds.

To produce a type of prototype requires intention, and although intention in design and craft is often focused on an artefact (be that an object, process or service), to arrive at the destination requires engagement with the experiential prototype. The essential nature of the prototype as experience is convergence—the convergence of many diverse minds and bodies into a unified whole. This journey and its outcomes can be imagined in most situations, but Constance Adams, like Bruce and Baxter, reminds us that it cannot be completely imagined in all situations. Yet despite this, imagining unknown territory and the mending of imaginary improbable situations is a necessary act. Drawing on her experience as a space architect for the NASA Mars 'Design Reference Mission', Adams comments on the astonishing rate with which humanity is advancing our entire species, and she reminds us of the necessity of collaboration in our global quest for greater understanding of our planet Earth. Adams argues that we run the risk 'of stumbling into a profound ignorance in body-based knowledge—that is, the understanding of balance, form and purpose that is learned by working with one's hands'. In raising this critical conflict, she considers our 'human relationship with tools and form-making in terms of *Homo sapiens astronauticus*' and offers a proposition about the future from the perspective of the international space astronaut. In this discussion, prototyping is considered as the mission to Mars itself as well as the process of preparing for a return journey into outer space twenty years hence. It is an extreme and unfamiliar context for discussing design and craft but one that helps us to acknowledge (or at least begin to acknowledge) the implications of biodiversity and reconsider what we perceive as useful in our skills development as well as our strategic decision making.

Rethinking our thinking is encouraged through *Prototype* in a general sense and in relation to design and craft. To varying degrees, each author looks at this issue. The historian Frederic Schwartz is arguably the only one who attends to the problem of the prototype, its relation to craft and design and what the logical and temporal conundrum of the prototype can offer thinking in general. Schwartz gives an account of certain theoretical and philosophical thoughts about craft and its most utopian futures—futures now past, including the notion of craft as being premodern; it is as much a way of thinking as a historical fact, an unfamiliar idea whose meaning unfolds through the complex dialogue of Prototopia. The reason for mentioning this is not to elevate Schwartz's essay but to acknowledge the different ways in which the concept of change and the process of innovation are considered; it is offered as a framework for rethinking design and craft and their relationships.

All of the essays in this volume offer a general overview of the prototype and its history as well as specific reference to the development of prototype(s) in contemporary life, yet none of them mimics or duplicates each other. In having a range of frameworks with which to consider and reconsider 'things', we give support to the process of evaluating the integrity of an idea (be it a process or product) and achieving excellence. The range of essays suggests the very idea that the prototype is a flexible, experimental tool, and even the most pragmatically conceived prototype carries some trace of utopian conviction—a suggestion of the way things might soon be different.

FURTHER READING

Bonanni, L., and Parkes, A. (2010), 'Virtual Guilds: Collective Intelligence and the Future of Craft', *The Journal of Modern Craft*, 3/2: 179–90.

Bonanni, L., Parkes, A., and Ishii, H. (2008), 'Future Craft: How Digital Media is Transforming Product Design', in *CHI '08 CHI Conference on Human Factors in Computing Systems Extended Abstracts on Human Factors in Computing Systems* Florence, Italy, 5–10 April 2008, New York: ACM, 2553–64.

Calaprice, A. (ed.) (2005), *The New Quotable Einstein*, Princeton, NJ: Princeton University Press.

Chicks on Speed (2010), *Don't Fashion Art Music*, London: Booth-Clibborn Editions and Dundee Contemporary Arts.

Dunne, A. (2005), *Hertzian Tales: Electronic Products, Aesthetic Experience, and Critical Design*, Cambridge, MA: MIT Press.

Maeda, J. (2006), *The Laws of Simplicity*, Cambridge, MA: MIT Press.

Maeda, J., and Bermont, B. (2011), *Redefining Leadership*, Cambridge, MA: MIT Press.

Valentine, L. (2004), 'The Activity of Rhetoric in the Process of a Designer's Thinking', PhD thesis, University of Dundee, Scotland.

Veiteberg, J. (2005), *Craft in Transition*, Bergen, Norway: Bergen National Academy of the Arts.

INDEX

The annotation of an italicized "f" or "t" indicates a reference to a figure or table on the specified page.